Brimming with creative inspiration, how-to projects, and useful information to enrich your everyday life, Quarto Knows is a favorite destination for those pursuing their interests and passions. Visit our site and dig deeper with our books into your area of interest: Quarto Creates, Quarto Cooks, Quarto Homes, Quarto Lives, Quarto Drives, Quarto Explores, Quarto Gifts, or Quarto Kids.

© 2019 Quarto Publishing Group USA Inc.
Text © 2017 Lisa Eldred Steinkopf
Photography © 2017, 2019 Chelsea Steinkopf, except as noted otherwise

This edition was published in 2019, first published in 2017 by Cool Springs Press, an imprint of The Quarto Group, 100 Cummings Center, Suite 265-D, Beverly, MA 01915 USA.
T (612) 344-8100
F (612) 344-8692
QuartoKnows.com

Cool Springs Press titles are also available at discount or retail, wholesale, promotional, and bulk purchase. For details, contact the Special Sales Manager by email at specialsales@quarto.com or by mail at The Quarto Group, Attn: Special Sales Manager, 100 Cummings Center, Suite 265-D, Beverly, MA 01915 USA.

10 9 8 7 6 5 4 3 2 1

ISBN: 978-0-7603-6592-2

Originally filed under the following
Library of Congress Cataloging-in-Publication Data

Names: Steinkopf, Lisa Eldred, 1966- author.
Title: Houseplants : the complete guide to choosing, growing, and caring for indoor plants / Lisa Eldred Steinkopf.
Description: Minneapolis, MN : Cool Springs Press, 2017. | Includes index.
Identifiers: LCCN 2017019287 | ISBN 9781591866909 (pb)
Subjects: LCSH: House plants. | Indoor gardening.
Classification: LCC SB419 .S7275 2017 | DDC 635.9--dc23
LC record available at https://lccn.loc.gov/2017019287

Cover Design: Evelin Kasikov
Page Design, Layout, and Illustration: Evelin Kasikov

Printed in China

MIX
Paper from responsible sources
FSC® C008047
www.fsc.org

PHOTO CREDITS

Crystal Liepa: 19 (bottom)

GAP Photos: 6, 50, 57, 104, 117, 133, 137, 139, 140, 142, 148, 151, 155

Shutterstock: 1, 19 (top right and middle left), 31, 34, 38, 40, 43, 45, 52, 54, 62, 77, 83, 84, 87, 100, 118, 125, 129, 144, 145, 173, 182, 195, 197

HOUSE
PLANTS

A GUIDE TO
CHOOSING AND CARING
FOR INDOOR PLANTS

LISA ELDRED STEINKOPF

COOL
SPRINGS
PRESS

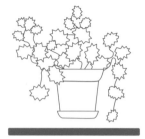

INTRODUCTION

We all have the need to nurture and care for other living things. Maybe you aren't ready for a cat, dog, or fish, but bringing home a houseplant can fulfill that need. Place a plant on the windowsill, and it will add living beauty to your home. Houseplants ask for so little but add so much life to a home. The care of that green friend falls solely on the owner. Our hope is that this book can help you keep your green roommate alive, healthy, and vibrant.

There is no such thing as a natural green thumb. Many believe either you are born with one or not. Yet, having a green thumb is just a matter of paying attention to the needs of your plants and noticing when they are trying to tell you something. Growing beautiful plants are easy if you have the time and pay attention to their specific needs.

Time restraints are popular excuses as to why someone has no plants in their home. One easy plant can take less than five minutes a week to care for, and the benefits it brings will lead to a desire for more greenery in your life. Liking and being successful with plants has more rewards than are always apparent. Plants have been proven to clean the air around us. B. C. Wolverton, a NASA scientist, conducted many experiments in the 1980s and found that plants remove VOCs—volatile organic chemicals—from our indoor environments. These chemicals can come from carpets, paint, manufactured furniture, household cleaning products, and more. One plant can remove most of the VOCs from a 100-square-foot (9.29 m²) area.

An important aspect of owning houseplants is the undeniable therapy that caring for plants affords us. Slowing down to care for something that is dependent on us can be therapeutic. Pick up a plant, remove dead leaves, check the growing medium for water, and wash the leaves with a soft cloth or sponge. One plant may become many more when the time it takes to care for one plant isn't enough to untangle the knots from the day. Many professional people own large collections of plants for just this reason. As Elvin McDonald wrote in his book, *Plants as Therapy*, "I believe that plants have enormous potential for maintaining emotional stability and . . . improving the lives of human beings." Nothing truer could be said.

Quite often, if you have a problem with a houseplant, you search online for information and help. But not every piece of information floating around on the Internet is true or pertinent to the specific plant for which you are caring. The information in this book will dispel the myths and misinformation about successfully raising houseplants. Plant societies are another good source of information. If you wish to learn as much as you can about a family of plants, such as cacti and other succulents, orchids, or African violets, join a plant society in your area. Joining a plant group can help you find like-minded people who don't tune out when you talk nonstop about your plants.

It is my hope this book will give you the confidence you need to bring a plant or two home to improve your environment and give it a warmer, more comfortable feeling that will bring joy to those who enter.

PLANTING

In every houseplant owner's life, the time comes to get your hands dirty. Plants grow, increase in size, and eventually need to be moved to a new container. In certain situations, it may mean the plant is moved into a similar-size container, returned to the same container, or moved into a larger container.

This process is one that can be enjoyable, knowing that you are helping your plant grow better. Providing it with the best potting medium for its particular needs ensures the root system can function well and provide the plant with what it requires for optimal growth. Repotting or up-potting are easy tasks, if done correctly and at the right time for the plant. Assess the needs of the plant you are working with. Is it root-bound? Is it looking undernourished or off-color? Does it need a new, clean pot or a different color pot to match your décor? Keep in mind the container size you need for your plant when shopping for a new pot. Measuring the old container to determine the size needed can be helpful before purchasing a new one. If up-potting a plant, make sure this is being done at a time when the plant is actively growing. The plant will thank you by pushing out new, healthy growth.

POTTING SUPPLIES

Before getting started, make sure all the supplies you need are at hand.

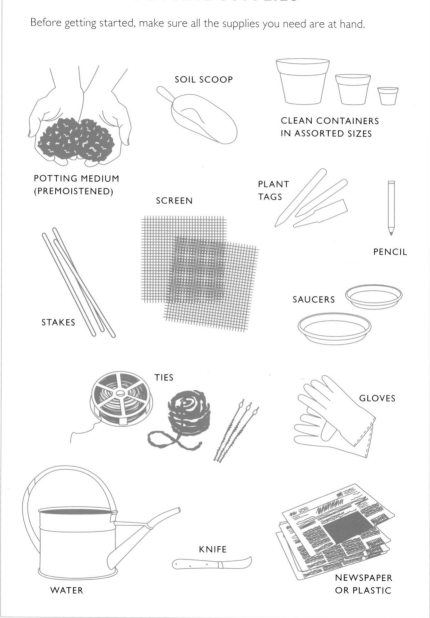

POTTING MEDIUM
(PREMOISTENED)

SOIL SCOOP

CLEAN CONTAINERS
IN ASSORTED SIZES

SCREEN

PLANT
TAGS

PENCIL

STAKES

SAUCERS

TIES

GLOVES

WATER

KNIFE

NEWSPAPER
OR PLASTIC

Repotting and Up-Potting

Repotting most often involves moving a plant from the utilitarian grower's pot to a more decorative pot of the same size. Inspect the roots when repotting. If the pot is full of roots and seems root-bound, you may have to repot in a larger container. Also, check that the depth of the plant in the potting medium is correct. Quite often, the stems are buried in ½ to 1 inch (1.27 to 2.54 cm) of extra soil. Remove the superfluous soil and pot the plant at a better depth.

Repotting is also necessary if your pot gets broken or you notice an accumulation of salt residue on the pot rim.

When up-potting, or moving your plant to a larger container, do it gradually. If you are moving a plant from a 4-inch (10.16 cm) pot, move up to a 6-inch (15.24 cm) pot, and so on. If a plant has too much soil surrounding its rootball, it may cause the roots to rot, as they cannot use all the water available to them.

▲ When up-potting, only change to a pot the next size up, unless the plant is extremely root-bound. You may well up-pot a plant many times during its lifetime.

▲ The roots have grown through the holes in the bottom of the pot. To successfully remove the plant, it may be necessary to cut the roots off, cut off the pot, or break the pot.

▲ This *Pilea involucrate* 'Norfolk' is residing in its utilitarian grower's pot and will be moved into the decorative pot on the right.

Houseplant Containers

▲ You can choose from a never-ending array of containers to hold your houseplants.

▶ This rooster planter was a vase, but with a drainage hole drilled in the bottom, it makes a perfect planter.

▲ Bulbous pots are not recommended. They make it extremely hard to remove a plant from the pot as its opening is smaller than the middle.

▲ Before planting, place a piece of screen over the hole to let water out but keep the potting medium in.

The only requirement of any container is proper drainage, meaning a drainage hole, not gravel in the bottom of the pot. Using gravel or pebbles as drainage is unnecessary and not helpful. Using medium all the way to the bottom of the container will make a long column of planting medium, which gives the plant more room for roots. Before adding the soil, place window screening over the hole; the potting medium will stay in and the excess water will easily drain out.

How to Adapt Pots for Planting

If you have a container without a drainage hole, it can be used as a *cachepot* (pronounced *cash-poe*), which is French for "flowerpot holder." If I had a pot I didn't want to drill a hole in, such as an antique piece of pottery, I would go this route. Water the plant in the sink, allow the excess water to drain from the bottom of the planting pot, and return the plant to the cachepot. Or, if the plant is too large, water the plant in the cachepot and use a turkey baster to suck out any extra water in the bottom.

If, on the other hand, you want to drill a hole in a container, I suggest buying a masonry drill bit or a diamond-tipped drill bit. These bits, especially the diamond bit, make it a breeze to drill a hole in any vessel, even glass. Wear safety glasses and follow the directions provided with the bit.

When finished repotting, use a pencil to write the common name and botanical name of the plant, as well as the date it was repotted on a plastic plant tag. You would be amazed how fast time goes by. You may find a plant seems to be struggling because it has been more than five years since the plant has been repotted. You may also find it useful to record the place it was purchased, the price paid, and the date purchased.

STEP 1 Choose either a masonry bit or diamond-tipped drill bit to make a hole in your container.

STEP 2 This pot has the hole one-half drilled through the container using a ¼-inch (0.64 cm) diamond-tipped drill bit.

STEP 3 The hole has been completely drilled through the container.

2

WATERING

Watering practices are the biggest killer of plants. Of course, the environment the plant is residing in makes a difference: the light the plant receives, the temperature of the home, and the humidity all play a part in the watering regime. It is recommended to practice checking your plants on a schedule.

The best way to check your houseplant for moisture is to stick your finger into the potting medium. If it is moist at the first or second knuckle, put the watering can down. If it is dry, then give it a good drink. Keeping it consistently moist is a better practice.

Every plant has different water needs, but the technique is the same for all. Giving your plant just a little water, hoping you don't overwater your plant, is not the correct way to water. Water *every* plant until water runs out the bottom of the pot. Make sure to water all the way around the pot, not consistently in one spot every time. This ensures that the whole rootball is well moistened. The key to thorough watering is the amount of time that passes before you water again. The point is, every plant is different, and each one needs to be checked individually to see if it needs water.

3

LIGHTING AND SPECIALTIES

Placing your plant in the correct light is one of the most important factors of successful indoor gardening. Since plants make their own nutrients in conjunction with the sun, the source of light is of optimum importance. The act of taking light, water, and carbon dioxide and changing it into nutrition is called *photosynthesis*, which takes place only in the green part of a plant. The good news for all life on earth is that oxygen is released as a byproduct of the photosynthetic process.

Determining the amount of light a specific plant needs is not always easy, and you may experience a few casualties while figuring out the best situations for your plants.

Light is measured in units called *foot candles*, which measure the amount of light visible to the human eye and are defined as the measure of light a candle casts on a surface one foot (0.3 m) away. Humans see much less of the light spectrum than plants. We see the green-yellow part of the spectrum, whereas plants use the red and blue parts. If you have a smartphone, there are apps you can download to let you know how many foot candles there are where you would like to place you plant. I'm not sure of their accuracy, so instead, let's talk about the window orientations in our homes and the plants they can support.

◀ If you have a sunroom or another space with windows on three sides of the room, you will be able to nurture most types of houseplants easily.

▼ West-facing windows can be quite hot in late afternoon, making them ideal for cactus and other warm-climate succulents.

◀ Window shades allow you to control light conditions as needed. If you are in an apartment with only western exposure, for example, shades will let you dim the harsh afternoon sunlight to prevent burning.

▼ Plants tend to grow toward the light. This is called *phototropism*. To prevent this, turn your plants a quarter turn every time you water.

▲ Sensitive plants prone to leaf burning, such as ferns, often do best in east-facing windows where they receive morning sun.

▲ Plants hung high in a window receive less sun than those on a windowsill or ledge.

▲ Skylights typically emit sunlight for most of the day, making them the spot for sun-loving plants or to pep up plants languishing in dim conditions.

▲ Mirrors and white walls can help plants in otherwise dim conditions by reflecting what little light there is.

▲ Incandescent lights, often used in conjunction with fluorescent lights, emit rather hot light and must be kept at some distance from plants. They encourage blooms, but don't do much for foliage.

▲ Electric lights are often necessary for blooming indoor plants, such as African violets.

◀ Newer LED lights can be much smaller and cost-efficient than the fluorescent shop light fixtures we are familiar with.

SUNLIGHT

The four exposures—east, west, north, or south—in our homes have very specific types of light. It is extremely important to determine the orientation of your windows.

EASTERN EXPOSURE: The sun comes up in your window, casting a bright, warm light that will not burn your plants. This is referred to as medium light and always comes in at an angle.

WESTERN EXPOSURE: The sun goes down in your window. Western light is also a bright light, but is consistently hotter than the east. This light may support quite a few high-light plants if they are close to the window. The light also comes in at an angle, like the eastern exposure, and allows a large number of plants to be grown further from the window.

SOUTHERN EXPOSURE: This receives the most intense light throughout the day. Because the sun is high in the sky in summer, the light shines down at a sharp angle close to the window. This means plants that need less sun can be placed higher or hung near the window. It is a strong light, though. If plants are moved a few feet from a south window, or there is a sheer curtain hung, a larger variety of plants can be placed in the southern exposure. As the sun is lower in the sky in winter, east and west window plants may be moved to the south window so they receive better light. It is also not as harsh as in summer.

The east and west exposures aren't affected as much by the seasons, as the sun comes in at an angle coming up and setting all through the year.

NORTHERN EXPOSURE: This never receives any direct sunlight and can support only low-light foliage plants. These plants are the ones usually found on the rain forest floor, where they live happily in the shade with just dappled light. Blooming plants are not a consideration for the north window unless you add supplemental light, which we will talk about later.

SKYLIGHT: This is a fifth exposure. The light will work its way across the floor as the sun moves across the sky, but will also add light to the whole room.

BAY WINDOW: This lets plants receive light from three exposures. If the window is on the north side, you have the added bonus of east and west exposure, and that changes the light your plants are getting. Growing blooming plants has now become possible.

GARDEN WINDOWS: These are mini greenhouses that make growing a larger variety of plants possible, even if it is a small area.

What are some indicators that your plant is receiving too little light?

• leaning into the light
• new growth may be pale with small leaves
• plants may stretch and lose their shape
• root rot, as the plant cannot use
  all the water it is given

On the other hand, plants can let you know they are receiving too much light, indicated by:

• wilting
• curling its leaves down toward the container
• sunburn

If these problems are ignored for too long, plants can eventually be stunted so severely they may not recover. Watch your plants closely and listen to what they tell you.

ELECTRIC LIGHT

Electric light makes it possible to grow plants without a window or to grow more plants when windowsill space runs out. There are three aspects of electric light: quality, duration, and intensity.

1 **QUALITY** of light refers to the color. Light is made up of the colors of the rainbow. The colors plants use are red and blue. The red light allows the plant to form flowers, and the blue light helps foliage grow and stay compact.

2 **DURATION** is the length of time a plant gets light in the day.

3 **INTENSITY** refers to the amount of light a plant receives. It is hard for our human eyes to determine this, but your plants will let you know if they are not happy with the intensity of light.

Photoperiodism is the reaction plants have to the length of days and nights. Short-day plants need short days and long nights (at least 12 hours) to bloom. Long-day plants need long days and short nights to bloom.

Day-neutral plants do not need a short day or long day to grow well or flower. The equal hours of light and dark suit them.

There are many types of electric light, but only a few are suitable for houseplants.

Fluorescent lights are the most common fixtures used with houseplants. They run cooler than incandescent bulbs and have a broader spectrum of light.

Using a cool white bulb paired with a warm white bulb covers both the blue and red spectrum needed for flowering and foliage health. There are also daylight and full-spectrum bulbs that have everything a plant needs in one bulb. Pair one of those bulbs with a regular fluorescent bulb, as the specialty bulbs are more expensive.

Fluorescent lights do need to be quite close to the plants, which may not be ideal if you want to grow taller plants. Plants grown under lights have to be approximately the same size. For flowering plants, the lights are usually placed 6 to 12 inches (15.2 to 30.5 cm) above the plants and for foliage plants, 12 to 24 inches (30.5 to 70 cm).

LED lights are the newest lights for the indoor gardener. Compared to fluorescent lights they are more efficient. Though they cost more, they are more cost-effective in the long run. The lights come in red and blue, which unfortunately turn your growing area pink. It is good for your plants, but many do not like how the pink color makes the plants appear. Fortunately, LED lights are becoming more available in white, allowing plants to receive both color waves they need. LED lights can be placed farther away from the plants, so taller plants can be grown under them.

I'll mention metal halide, mercury discharge, and low- and high-pressure sodium lights briefly, as not many houseplant growers use them. They are usually used for lighting a very large area and, quite often, in commercial situations or for cannabis production.

When using artificial light, make sure a reflector is used, which will guide the light downward to the plants. Also, make sure the lights and fixtures are dusted on a regular basis.

If you are using fluorescent lights, they need to be changed yearly, as they start losing their light intensity with age. The ends of the tubes eventually turn black and then need to be changed.

An important item in a light garden is a timer. Your plants will receive the same light every day without you having to remember to turn the lights on and off.

Whether you choose to only use sunlight or supplement with electric light, most importantly, watch your plants for their reactions. Move plants around until they seem happy in the light they are receiving.

PROPAGATION

There are many ways to propagate plants. Certain procedures work for some plants but not others. See the plant profiles (page 36) for the best procedure for a particular plant.

The most popular way to make more plants is *stem cutting*. Use a sharp knife or clippers for a clean cut. Cut the stem at an angle ¼ to 1 inch (0.6 to 2.5 cm) below a node. If you are taking a cutting of a succulent, allow the cutting to dry out for a few days and the end to callus over. Planting a cactus or other succulent cutting immediately after cutting may cause it to rot.

Leaf cuttings are another way plants are propagated. One leaf is all that is needed to make duplicate plants. Cut a leaf off, leaving at least a 1-inch (2.5 cm) petiole (the stalk that attaches the leaf to the stem). Insert the cutting into the potting media at a slant.

TIP: Cutting at an Angle

When cutting stems for propagation, cut them at an angle. If cut straight across, there is less area from which new roots can emerge. It doesn't have to be a perfect 45-degree angle; close enough is fine. The angled edge allows for more area to be in contact with the potting medium and to grow more roots.

◄ Three stem cuttings from ivy, jewel orchid, and pothos plants.

▲ A single leaf of many succulents can be simply placed on a pot of moist medium. They will eventually grow new plants.

STEP 1 Gather the supplies you will need to air layer your plant, including plastic wrap, a knife, a toothpick, moss, and twine.

STEP 2 Place a toothpick in the cut that has been made in the stem to hold it open.

STEP 3 Cut the toothpick so it doesn't put a hole in the plastic wrap that will surround the stem.

STEP 4 Wrap the cut area with damp sphagnum moss.

STEP 5 Encase the moss with plastic wrap.

How to Propagate

Many questions arise about what to do with an old, leggy plant. There is a solution called *air layering*. This process allows a plant to make a new set of roots while still attached to the parent plant, receiving water and nutrients. This process isn't a quick one, so patience is needed.

Choose the area where you would like the new roots to grow. If you prefer to shorten your plant to 1 or 2 feet (0.3 to 0.6 m) high, choose a spot that far from the top of the plant to work on. At that spot, use a knife to slice through the stem at an upward angle, only cutting approximately halfway through the stem. Place a toothpick or matchstick, depending on the size of the stem, in the cut to prop it open. Wrap damp sphagnum moss around that area and cover with plastic wrap.

Be sure to secure the plastic carefully at the top and bottom. This creates a miniature greenhouse around the cut. In approximately 4 to 6 months, roots will grow into the moss. When the roots are obvious to you, the plant can then be cut from the parent plant and be potted up in an appropriate potting media. The remaining plant can then be discarded, or cut the stem lower and it may sprout a new plant from that cut point, giving you two plants.

Making new plants from old is a wonderful way to share plants with others. Plants make excellent gifts, and most people are thrilled to receive them. If you join a plant society, the members are very generous and more than happy to share their prize plants with others.

STEP 6 Tie the top and bottom with twine, completely enclosing the moss in plastic wrap so it will stay damp.

STEP 7 When completed, the cut area is enclosed with plastic, like a miniature greenhouse. When the roots fill the plastic wrap, it can be removed and the top of the leggy plant can be cut off and planted. The plant will be approximately 1 foot (0.3 m) tall.

TERRARIUMS

Terrariums can be used to grow plants we would otherwise have a difficult time growing in our homes. They keep humidity-loving plants happy and healthy. If you keep your house a little on the cold side, terrariums keep your plants warm. Most plants that are appropriate for terrariums are medium-light plants. Your terrarium should be placed in a bright area without direct sun. If your plants suffer from your sporadic watering practices, terrariums are almost self-sufficient once established.

What are the steps to making a terrarium? The container is the first thing to contemplate. Think about what you want the final product to look like and the plants you want to use. Choosing a larger container will greatly expand your selection of plants. Choose a clear container— colored containers, even lightly tinted ones, do not allow sufficient light through. Make sure the container has a lid, which allows the moisture to remain in the enclosure. Some of the containers used back in the 1970s looked alien. Today, the possibilities are endless.

Clean and shine the container before planting, and be careful as you add soil and plants so as not to get the container dirty. Choose plants that will fit your container for the greatest length of time. Many small terrarium plants are seedlings of plants that will eventually become very large. It will be some time before this happens, but if you can find actual miniature plants, your terrarium will last longer without

a lot of trimming. Because of the fairy gardening craze, there are plenty of mini plants out there.

Choose an appropriate soil for the plants you are using. A quality, fast-draining houseplant soil will be sufficient for most. The size of your container and the size of your plants will determine the amount of soil used. Most often, a few inches of soil is all that is needed. Pebbles aren't needed for drainage in the bottom of the container, nor is charcoal to keep it "sweet." Make sure there is enough room for the roots of the plants. If the plants you want to use are too tall, slice the soil ball one-half way up in the middle and spread the rootball out to allow it to fit in your container without having to add as much soil. This will not injure your plants and will promote new root growth. Spread the medium in the container, making areas that are lower and higher for added interest.

Add your plants, making sure they aren't touching the sides of the container, as the leaves will rot as the humidity collects on the glass. Give your plants room for growth so trimming can be kept to a minimum. After they are planted, they need to be carefully watered. Add only enough water to moisten the soil. Your terrarium will need to be watched carefully for a few weeks after planting. If it gets too steamy, the cover may need to be tipped or taken off temporarily. Getting the atmosphere correct is a little tricky, but when it is balanced, you need only check it occasionally.

Now that the plants are in, it is time to add the details. The accoutrements available for terrariums are endless. They can be as simple as decorative rocks or sticks from your own yard, or more elaborate, like figurines and small gardening tools, gnomes, fairies, deer, or whatever you find that you like.

Now it's time to add a groundcover. This step can be skipped if you prefer the look of the soil. For a woodsy effect, small chips of orchid bark or moss work well. Small pebbles or decorative stones or glass pieces can be used as well.

▲ Classic terrariums use glass panel "Wardian"-style enclosures and are planted with a variety of plants to mimic the look of full-size conservatories. This terrarium features creeping fig, Neanthe bella palm, croton, ruffle fern, and club moss.

DISH GARDENS/
MINIATURE GARDENS

A dish garden is simply a grouping of plants in a container that all require approximately the same growing conditions. The newest craze is miniature or fairy gardens, and adding small accessories to your dish garden makes it fun. Kids love making these, so it is a great way to interest children in growing plants.

You can make your own version that will last a long time if you choose your plants carefully. Finding truly small houseplants can be challenging, but not impossible. Because of the miniature fairy and gnome gardening craze, garden centers began offering a large selection of plants appropriate for your small garden.

Buying plants with similar growing habits is very important. Do not mix cacti and other succulents with ferns, as the outcome will be bleak. Arid dish gardens containing cacti and other succulents are actually the best way to put these plants together. They do not belong in a terrarium, as the humidity is too high and will lead to rot.

Decide which kind of plants you will be using for your dish garden, and choose your potting medium accordingly. A cacti dish garden will need a fast-draining medium, while ferns and other foliage houseplants will need a heavier, water-retaining medium. The most important factor, though, is to have a drainage hole in whatever container you use.

◀ Tiny accessories added to a houseplant arrangement featuring small variety plants creates a quaint miniature garden.

WATER GARDENS

Growing plants in water alone is an increasingly popular practice, but it has been done for generations. Remember when your grandma had any amount of small "slips" of plants rooting in baby food jars on the windowsill? All types of plants can be grown in water. Even though plants left in too-wet potting medium may rot, they will grow fine if they are growing solely in water because water roots are different from soil roots. Cacti and other succulents can be grown in water alone. It is weird to think you can grow plants in water alone when they might not like to

be moist when grown in potting medium. Many people grow their plants in small clay balls made for hydroponic growing, and some just in decorative stones. There are decorative containers made just for rooting plants or growing them in water.

Change the water often to keep it clear. Any colored glass container can be used, but if a clear glass container is used, algae may grow. If this happens, move the container to a lower light area, or just change the water and clean the glass often. Watching the roots grow is half the fun.

◀ A water garden can be very simple, like this pothos cutting rooted into a small bottle of water and hung on a wall within a rustic picture frame.

▲ A shallow bowl filled with stones and water can be used to create a water garden—just be sure to change the water frequently.

BONSAI

Bonsai is Japanese for "potted plant." Bonsai plants may be generations old and are truly an artform. The traditional plants used for bonsai are outdoor plants that need a cool season, such as maple trees and evergreens. Using tropical or houseplants is a newer concept, but a faster way to achieve an ancient-looking tree without the complication of winter care. These small, confined trees are quite labor-intensive and because of their small root systems, may need to be watered every day. If you leave on a vacation, you may need to find a bonsai sitter.

Many plants can be used for this ancient art, but the most often used are ficus varieties. You can start your own from a small plant or buy one already trained into a beautiful shape that only needs maintenance to keep its shape. These are not inexpensive plants, but well worth it in the long run.

Starting your own from a small plant and training it into the shape you prefer can be therapeutic. The shapes the plants are trained to take are many. Some cascade over the pot and can be displayed on a pedestal; some are groves of trees that look like they've been growing forever; and others take serpentine shapes. Shaping these plants requires soft copper wire and special tools to trim them correctly. Joining a local bonsai club in your area or online will give you the information and a like-minded community you may need to succeed with your bonsai.

◀ ▶ Bonsai plants are carefully trimmed to create the look of miniature trees. Ficus plants are commonly used, but there are many other plants that can be used as well.

VERTICAL GARDENS
OR LIVING WALLS

Growing plants on a vertical plane is a newer trend and is a way to maximize space. Many living walls seen outside are made with pallets. There are a number of wall setups that are easy to use and are perfect for houseplants. They are waterproof and have catch basins to collect water run-off, as water running down the wall into your carpet is not ideal. The key, as with all houseplants, is to find a place in your home that can meet the plants' need for light. There has to be enough illumination so the plants do not reach too much for light, as these gardens can't be rotated as freestanding plants can. This problem can be solved by placing an electric grow light over the top of the living wall.

Find the system that will work best for your area. The original living walls were called wall pockets and are now a collectible item from the early to mid-part of the twentieth century. There are still pots made today that hang on the wall and are designed for a single plant. There are also systems that can hold a multitude of plants. The key to a multiple plant system is to choose plants that are compatible as far as light and water conditions. Use all low- to medium-light plants together or all high-light plants. Do not mix cacti and other succulents with ferns. Not only do they not have the same light requirements, they don't have the same moisture or humidity requirements either. Do a little research so you aren't setting yourself up for failure. A living wall is a beautiful piece of art, if grown well.

◄ Upcycled containers hung on a wall are used to create an interesting vertical garden.

▶ A variety of small plants are tucked into various crevices of this living wall planter. This planting includes bromeliads, begonias, philodendrons, and anthurium.

4

PLANT
PROFILES

In this section, we will cover the care of individual houseplants. They are broken into three groups: easy to grow, moderately easy to grow, and challenging to grow. The houseplants considered challenging may not necessarily be that much harder to grow than an easy or moderately easy plant, but just need more attention. If you don't have the time and want to make sure your plant thrives without too much effort, choose a plant from the easy to grow section. If you like a challenge and have the time and inclination, try one in the challenging section. Of course, everyone's growing conditions are different, and you may find that a plant in the challenging section is super easy for you to grow. These are categorized as to how I have found them to grow in my experience and growing conditions.

No matter which one or more you share your home with, hopefully they thrive and make you happy—which is all that really matters anyway. Remember, killing a plant is only a learning experience and shouldn't discourage you from trying again. There is a plant out there for every home and growing condition. Happy growing!

AIR PLANT

BOTANICAL NAME: *Tillandsia*

In their native habitats, air plants grow on trees and are epiphytes, which are plants that grow on other plants but are not parasitic. They only use them for a place to rest and take nothing from the host plant. They are easy, versatile plants that have taken the houseplant world by storm. The ease of care, accessible cost, and versatility make this a plant for everyone. Though these plants are commonly called air plants, they do need water to live. They naturally live in places with high humidity, but in our heated, low-humidity homes, they will definitely need to be watered—in their case, soaked—on a regular basis.

LIGHT PREFERENCE: Air plants need a bright light to do their best. An east or west window works and some may appreciate a south window. If light is at appropriate levels, they will flower and send out babies.

WATERING: Soak air plants once a week in tepid water for approximately 30 minutes, drain upside-down for a short time, and return them to their growing area. Some recommend distilled water, but tap water works as long as its chemical content isn't high. These plants naturally grow on an angle, so water never sits in the middle of the plant. If it does, the plant may rot and fall apart. Like any plant, the more light they receive, the more water they will use. They love humid air, so a home in the kitchen or bathroom is perfect, if there is enough light.

FLOWER: The small flowers are brightly colored, often with purple flowers, and protrude from colorful bracts.

SIZE: This large family of plants ranges in size from under 1 inch (2.5 cm) to 3 feet (0.9 m) and more.

PROPAGATION: As the plants grow and mature, they will send out offsets—"babies" or "pups"—from their base. When these new plants are approximately one-third the size of the parent, they can be removed. If preferred, they can be left on the parent plant, and a large clump of plants will form.

CULTIVARS: There are many varieties of air plants out there, and many are easy to grow in the house.

• *TILLANDSIA IONANTHA*—The most common air plant sold to consumers, it may reach 2 to 3 inches (5.1 to 7.6 cm) tall and sends out plenty of offsets at its base with enough light and appropriate water.

• *T. USNEOIDES*—Dripping from trees in the south, Spanish moss is an icon of that region. Many people don't realize it is a living plant because dried Spanish moss is sold in craft stores for projects. It needs to be soaked the same as the other tillandsias and hung to dry. It is a light green/gray color when living and turns brown when dead.

• *T. XEROGRAPHICA*—The Greek word *xeros* means to dry. These large plants naturally grow in dry forests of Mexico and enjoy full sun. These need less water and more sun than other tillandsias, so be careful not to overwater and rot them. If in intense light, they will need more water than if in a medium light. They may not need to be soaked weekly like the other members of the family.

• *T. TECTORUM*—This fuzzy-looking tillandsia can be grown in high light and actually prefers it. The fuzzy silver covering helps protect it from the sun in its native habitat. It loves extremely high humidity to go along with the high light. This is a very striking plant.

ALOE VERA

BOTANICAL NAME: *Aloe vera*
(*Aloe barbadensis* syn.)

The medicinal properties of *Aloe vera* are touted extensively and for good reason. Have you ever burnt your finger and found the amazing relief that using aloe gave you? It also soothes and cools a sunburn. The great thing is that you can grow your own! This is a succulent that is easy to grow in bright light, and it sends out many offsets, making it easy to share with friends and family.

LIGHT PREFERENCE: Give this plant bright light. If you have a place on your south or west windowsill, they will grow well. If placed in direct, unobstructed light, you may see it flower. If summered outside, they can sunburn, so acclimate them first, gradually moving them to high light.

WATERING: This juicy succulent does not need a lot of water, so keep the medium on the dry side. Make sure your aloe is in a fast-draining porous medium, and never leave it standing in water.

FLOWER: With enough light, long stems and yellow tubular flowers will appear. It is unlikely that they will flower in your home.

SIZE: The leaves may reach up to 2 feet (0.6 m) tall.

PROPAGATION: Aloes send out large numbers of "babies" or offsets at the base of the parent plant. They can be easily separated from the mother and potted up individually.

ALUMINUM PLANT

BOTANICAL NAME: *Pilea cadierei*

The aluminum plant is named for its shiny, quilted leaves. The surface splotches are a shiny silver and look like aluminum. The colorful leaves of the pilea add a welcome respite to an all-green grouping of plants. If your plant gets leggy, as they often do, take cuttings and start new plants.

LIGHT PREFERENCE: Keep it in bright light, such as in an east or west window. It does not like full sun.

WATERING: Keep it evenly moist, never standing in water, and plant in a well-drained potting medium. Keep the humidity up by setting the plant on a pebble tray. With enough light, this plant will do well in a terrarium.

FLOWER: It does produce small clusters of white flowers held a couple inches above the foliage. It may not bloom in your home environment, but is grown for its foliage anyway.

SIZE: It usually reaches 12 to 15 inches (30.5 to 38.1 cm).

PROPAGATION: Pilea is easily propagated from tip cuttings rooted in moist potting medium.

ANGEL VINE, MATTRESS VINE

BOTANICAL NAME: *Muehlenbeckia complexa*

Angel vine is an exuberant grower, covering a topiary frame quickly and effectively, which is why it is often used for such supports. Its diminutive leaves and wiry stems give an airy look to any planter. It works well as a groundcover around a specimen plant in a large pot.

LIGHT PREFERENCE: Angel vine prefers bright light but can tolerate and grow moderately well in a lower light. An east or west exposure is preferred, but a north window would work well, too.

WATERING: Keep this vine well-watered. If it is allowed to dry out, all the leaves may fall off. If you are lucky to catch it soon after, rehydrating it may bring it back.

FLOWER: It develops small cream-colored flowers that are quite inconspicuous, but only with enough light.

SIZE: The small-leaved vine may seem dainty and diminutive, but its other common name of mattress vine indicates its true nature. In its native habitat, this plant is a rampant groundcover. In our homes, it may reach 3 to 4 feet (0.9 to 1.2 m) long, maybe more. If used as a topiary plant, either keep winding it around the frame or keep it in shape by pruning.

PROPAGATION: Root tip cuttings in a moist potting medium. The leaves are thin, so covering the cuttings with plastic or glass will keep the humidity up while they are rooting.

ARROWHEAD VINE

BOTANICAL NAME: *Syngonium podophyllum*

When you purchase this plant, it may not be apparent that it is a vine as characteristic may take a while to develop. Its most attractive factor is its arrowhead-shaped leaves that range in color from silver to green to pink and any or all of those colors mixed together.

LIGHT PREFERENCE: Place in a bright light and turn frequently as it tends to lean toward the light in a short span of time. The thin leaves will not appreciate an overly bright light, as they may sunburn.

WATERING: Keep the arrowhead evenly moist and place on a pebble tray for extra humidity. Allowing the plant to dry out or allowing the humidity to drop too low may cause the leaf edges and tips to brown.

FLOWER: They may develop a small white spadix or small spike of flowers surrounded by a white spathe or sheathing bract, but rarely in the home.

SIZE: Until it begins to vine, the plant is only 12 to 18 inches (30.5 to 45.7 cm) tall. Once it starts vining, it could reach up to 3 feet (0.9 m). They can be trained to grow up a mossy pole or trellis or can be trimmed to keep it smaller.

PROPAGATION: Take 6- to 8-inch (15 to 20 cm) tip cuttings and root in a moist potting medium. Because of their thin leaves and love of humidity, covering the cuttings while rooting may be helpful.

CULTIVARS:

• **'MOONSHINE'**—This variety is a light silver in color.

• **'WHITE BUTTERFLY'**—One of the most popular varieties available, with light green leaves edged in dark green.

• **'PINK SPLASH'**—A variety with pink markings scattered on medium green leaves.

• **'MINI PIXIE'**—A miniature white and green variety that may only grow to 3 inches (7.6 cm), perfect for a terrarium or fairy garden.

• **'PINK FAIRY'**—A miniature variety that is pink in color and stays approximately 3 inches (7.6 cm) tall.

ASPARAGUS FERN

BOTANICAL NAME: *Asparagus densiflorus* 'Sprengeri'

This popular plant, while not a true fern, is often grouped with them. It is an airy plant with arching stems covered with small needle-like leaves. If grown as an individual plant, it will surprise you with how fast it will fill the pot. The thin leaves may yellow and fall off when under stress, such as a change in light, temperature, or moisture.

LIGHT PREFERENCE: Give it bright light but not full sun. The plant will yellow in full sun and if it is under-fertilized, as it is a heavy feeder. The roots of the plant are very large and fleshy, and like water and a regular fertilizer schedule.

WATERING: Keep it well-watered; if under-watered, it may drop a lot of needles/leaves.

FLOWER: It produces small white flowers, which excludes it from the fern family. Ferns do not produce seeds (which come from flowers), but instead produce minute spores. The flowers turn into red berries that eventually turn black.

SIZE: There are several varieties ranging from 2 feet (0.6 m) to more than 4 feet (1.2 m).

PROPAGATION: The easiest way to make more of these plants is to separate the rootball. This can be accomplished by using a knife to cut apart the sections or pull the fleshy roots (tubers) apart and then plant them up individually.

CULTIVARS:

• **FOXTAIL FERN (*ASPARAGUS DENSIFLORUS*)** 'Meyeri'—This cultivar has stems that resemble upright foxtails. They grow to 2 feet (0.6 m) tall.

• **ASPARAGUS FERN VINE (*A. SETACEUS*)**— This asparagus fern, with its airy, layered fronds, can grow as long as 10 feet (3 m) as it begins to vine. It can be trimmed to keep it compact.

BABY RUBBER PLANT

SIZE: It is rarely taller than 12 inches (30.5 cm).

PROPAGATION: Propagate by taking stem cuttings, or it can be propagated from a single leaf, like the African violet.

CULTIVAR:

• **RAINBOW PEPEROMIA** *(PEPEROMIA CLUSIIFOLIA)*—This peperomia resembles the baby rubber plant and is in the same family. This one has more pointed leaves and red color in the leaves. The care is essentially the same.

BOTANICAL NAME: *Peperomia obtusifolia*

The name leads one to believe we are talking about a rubber plant (or ficus), but the two aren't related. This member of the Piperaceae family is a true succulent plant and can take some neglect, unlike its other family members. It has small, rounded, rubbery leaves, and it also has a variegated version that is attractive.

LIGHT PREFERENCE: They prefer medium to bright light, which is especially important if the plant is variegated.

WATERING: Use a fast-draining potting medium for this succulent plant. Water thoroughly, then water again when it is quite dry.

FLOWER: The flowers are on a long, skinny 2- to 3-inch (5.1 to 7.6 cm) long spike resembling a rat tail. They are natural to the plant but hardly "attractive."

BIRD'S NEST SNAKE PLANT

BOTANICAL NAME: *Sansevieria trifasciata* 'Hahnii'

The snake plant is easily identified by its tall, spiky leaves. Another type of snake plant forms short rosettes of leaves resembling the round shape of bird's nests, thus the common name. They come in a range of colors from dark green to bright yellow, some with stripes and patches of variegation. These small plants are perfect for low-light and medium-light situations. The more variegation that is present on the leaves, the more light it will need to keep the colors vibrant.

LIGHT PREFERENCE: Snake plants are known for their tolerance of low light, especially the dark green varieties. If given a medium to bright light, they will do better.

WATERING: Keep this plant on the dry side, especially if it is placed in a low-light situation. If kept too wet, the plant will collapse due to rot. Do not leave water standing in the middle of the rosette for the same reason. If kept in medium to bright light, water when the planting medium is almost completely dry.

FLOWER: Older plants in enough light will send out a spray of white flowers, but that doesn't always happen in the conditions of a home setting.

SIZE: The bird's nest types can range from 4 inches (10.2 cm) to more than a foot (0.3 m) high. They will expand and spread out with the growth of the offsets from the base of the parent plant.

PROPAGATION: The easiest way to propagate this plant is to separate the offsets and plant them in their own container. A single leaf can also be cut into pieces, allowed to callus over and be planted in a moist medium. Make sure the leaf is placed so that the original bottom of the leaf is in the medium or it will not grow.

CULTIVARS:

- **'GOLDEN HAHNII'**—A golden variety with stripes of lighter yellow and green. This plant will not exceed 5 inches (12.7 cm) in height, but after a few years will send out offsets and may reach 8 to 10 inches (20.3 to 25.4 cm) or more, if not separated.

- **'BLACK STAR'**—The leaves are a dark green edged with yellow.

- **'JADE'**—A pure dark green variety.

- **'STARLITE'**—A gray leaf edged with yellow.

BISHOP'S CAP CACTUS OR STAR PLANT

BOTANICAL NAME: *Astrophytum ornatum*

From above, this cactus has a star shape that appears to spiral a bit. It's easy to grow, and the white felt scales on the body of the cactus give the plant a unique look. It is globe-shaped as a young plant but elongates with age. Make sure it is growing in a fast-draining medium to avoid rot.

LIGHT PREFERENCE: Give it a bright light such as a south-facing windowsill. If the light level is too low, the cactus will elongate excessively.

WATERING: Do not overwater this plant or allow it to sit in water. Too much water, or watering while the plant is sitting in a colder area, such as a windowsill, will cause the cactus to rot.

FLOWER: A pale yellow flower appears at the tip of this cactus but may not do so in the home environment.

SIZE: With age, it can become as tall as 30 inches (76.2 cm) or more, but most likely will not reach that size in the house.

PROPAGATION: Propagate by sowing seed (if not from the flowers of another plant, then purchased from a reputable seed supplier).

BLUE BEAR'S PAW FERN

BOTANICAL NAME: *Phlebodium aureum*

Your attention is first drawn to the large blue fronds of the fern. As you get closer, your attention is then stolen by the huge furry "caterpillars" creeping along the medium. These furry rhizomes (spreading stems) crawl across the potting medium, sending up fronds along the way. The thick, leathery fronds are more forgiving of the low humidity in our homes compared to most ferns. Give this fern plenty of room.

LIGHT PREFERENCE: It needs a medium light that would come from the east or back a couple of feet from a west window.

WATERING: Though it is forgiving of low humidity, do not let the potting medium dry out, but keep it evenly moist.

FLOWER: Ferns do not produce flowers.

SIZE: This fern demands some room. The fronds are up to 3 feet (0.9 m) tall, and the rhizomes need a low, wide pot to contain them. They will crawl up and over the pot rim when they hit the edge.

PROPAGATION: The spores that appear on the backside of the fronds can be sown in a moist medium and covered to keep the humidity high. You can also remove a piece of the rhizome with a frond attached and pin it to moist potting medium with a bent piece of wire; the medium needs to stay moist.

BUNNY'S EARS, POLKA DOT CACTUS

FLOWER: The flowers are a creamy yellow and are borne on the tips of the "bunny ears."

SIZE: They are usually under 18 inches (45.7 cm) tall.

PROPAGATION: Carefully remove a pad of the plant, allow it to dry and callus over, and then plant in a well-drained medium.

BOTANICAL NAME: *Opuntia microdasys*

This cute cactus may seem cuddly, as its names imply, but do not touch it without gloves. The spikes are really glochids that are very small barbed prickles. They attach to the skin and are quite painful; you may need tweezers to remove them. Many people use tape to pull them off, or they spread glue on the area, let it dry, and pull it off to remove the painful spikes. So why grow this plant? It is an endearing cactus, and the small tufts of glochids give it a polka-dot effect.

LIGHT PREFERENCE: Give this cactus as much light as you can, as it needs bright light to bloom.

WATERING: Plant this cactus in a well-drained soil. Water thoroughly and then allow the medium to dry down quite a bit before watering again. Do not allow the plant to stand in water. Keep it drier in the winter when the light levels are low.

CAST IRON PLANT

BOTANICAL NAME: *Aspidistra elatior*

This plant has been grown in dim parlors since the Victorian times, as it tolerates low light and adverse conditions.

LIGHT PREFERENCE: It can tolerate low light but would do well in medium light. The newer variegated cultivars need medium light to keep their variegation.

WATERING: It is also known for its tolerance to drying out, but prefers to be evenly moist. The less light it has, the less water it will need.

FLOWER: The flowers are borne at the base of the leaves on the soil, but they are not often seen in the home setting.

SIZE: The long, strappy leaves can be up to 2½ feet (0.8 m) long.

PROPAGATION: Separate sections of the plant and pot them up individually.

CULTIVARS:

- **'MILKY WAY'**—This is a speckled variety.

- **'VARIEGATA'**—This is a white-striped variety.

- **'SNOW CAP'**—This variety has white tips on the leaves.

CHINESE EVERGREEN

BOTANICAL NAME: *Aglaonema*

This group of plants is being hybridized at a rapid rate. They used to be available only in shades of green but now boast pinks, reds, and peach colors.

LIGHT PREFERENCE: The older hybrids, mostly green, can take low light and grow quite well. The newer colorful hybrids need medium light and do well in an east or west window. If placed in low light, they will lose their bright coloration.

WATERING: Let the soil dry down 1 to 2 inches (2.5 to 5.1 cm) before watering. They also prefer higher humidity, so place them on pebble trays.

FLOWER: *Aglaonema* with good light will flower, but as they are grown for their beautiful foliage, it benefits the plant to cut the flowers off. The flowering spadix is surrounded by a white spathe.

SIZE: The size ranges from 12 inches (30.5 cm) to approximately 3 feet (0.9 m).

PROPAGATION: *Aglaonema* can be propagated by stem cuttings or division.

CULTIVARS: These are just a few of the many cultivars now available. The newer ones have beautiful colors and markings.

- **'ANYANMANEE'**—Usually sold as Red Aglaonema in the stores, this cultivar has variegated dark pink leaves and grows 12 to 15 inches (30.5 to 38.1 cm) tall.

- **'CRETA'**—This cultivar has green leaves with red markings and grows 12 inches (30.5 cm) tall.

- **'EMERALD BEAUTY'**—This is one of the older varieties that can take low-light conditions. It has dark green leaves with light green mottled stripes and grows up to 24 inches (61 cm) tall.

- **'SILVER QUEEN'**—Also an older variety with opposite coloring of 'Emerald Beauty', this has light green leaves with dark green mottled stripes. It also can take lower-light conditions and will grow up to 18 inches (45.7 cm) tall.

- **'PINK DALMATIAN'**—This is a beautiful cultivar with pink splashes on dark green shiny leaves. It grows 12 to 18 inches (30.5 to 45.7 cm) tall.

- **'WHITE LANCE'**—The leaves of this unusual cultivar are only 1 inch (2.5 cm) wide and have a light gray color. It grows 18 inches (45.7 cm) tall.

- **'SPARKLING SARAH'**—This cultivar, which grows 12 to 15 inches (30.5 to 38.1 cm) tall, sports a pink midrib with pink veins on a bright green leaf.

COFFEE PLANT

BOTANICAL NAME: *Coffea arabica*

What a fun plant to grow! It really is the plant that produces coffee beans but will probably never produce enough to make a cup of coffee for you. The glossy green leaves with wavy edges make a gorgeous houseplant. It likes to stay warm and needs a bright spot to flower and produce the red berries. This plant does not like to be touched excessively, so place it out of high-traffic areas.

LIGHT PREFERENCE: Give it a bright spot for best results.

WATERING: Keep your coffee plant well-watered, but not standing in water. High humidity is necessary to keep the leaf edges from turning brown, so place the plant on a pebble tray.

FLOWER: Small white flowers grow along the branches, which then turn into red berries that contain the beans that are then roasted to make coffee.

SIZE: It may reach up to 4 feet (1.2 m) tall in the house unless kept pruned.

PROPAGATION: Take tip cuttings or plant the seeds.

COPPER SPOONS

BOTANICAL NAME: *Kalanchoe orgyalis*

The leaves of this unique plant are covered with a brown-colored fuzz that feels like velvet. As it ages, the color fades to a silver color. It is definitely a conversation piece if grown in a bright window, which gives it the best color. This is a great plant for kids, as they love to pet the soft leaves.

LIGHT PREFERENCE: Grow this colorful succulent in a south or west window for the best color and more compact growth. If grown in light that is too low, the plant will stretch and reach for the light.

WATERING: Grow in a fast-draining medium, as this succulent plant does not want to be waterlogged. After watering, let it almost completely dry out before watering again.

FLOWER: If given enough light, it may produce small, bright yellow flowers at the tip of the plant.

SIZE: It can grow up to 4 feet (1.2 m) tall but in the home may stay quite a bit smaller.

PROPAGATION: Take tip cuttings, but allow them to callus over before planting in a moist, fast-draining potting medium.

CORN PLANT

BOTANICAL NAME: *Dracaena fragrans*

The corn plant is aptly named as it does resemble the actual corn plant with its tall stature and strappy leaves. The corn plant is quite often used in office settings, as it can tolerate low light and some neglect. Yet, if well taken care of, it makes a dramatic statement in any room. Keep the long leaves dusted and clean for a more attractive, healthy specimen. When purchasing this plant, you will notice it usually has three different heights of woody stems, supporting a fountain of green at each tip. They are sold like that to make for a fuller container of greenery.

LIGHT PREFERENCE: As previously stated, this plant can tolerate low light but would prefer a medium to bright light, but not full sun.

WATERING: When watering this plant, it is important to water evenly over the entire potting medium to avoid rotting the canes. These canes can have small root systems and may need to be straightened after the plant is brought home and later as they settle in. Because they may lean, the canes need to be firmed in often. Be careful when straightening the canes to not firm the soil too much, compacting the medium and forcing the oxygen out. As they grow, the root systems will get larger and be better able to support the canes.

FLOWER: With sufficient light, these plants may send out their stems of white flowers, but not often in the home setting.

SIZE: The height can reach 6 feet (1.8 m) or more.

PROPAGATION: There are three ways the corn plant can be propagated. The tip of the plants can be cut and rooted to make new plants. This may become necessary to keep the plant at a shorter height. You can cut the tall brown cane to a shorter height, and new growth should push out of the sides of the cane near the top. The piece of cane you cut off can also be allowed to dry a bit and then placed in a moist potting medium and kept warm. Make sure the bottom of the cane is the part touching the medium and roots should form.

CULTIVARS:

- **'MASSANGEANA'**—A yellow stripe runs down the middle of the leaves.

- **'VICTORIA'**—The leaves of this cultivar are shorter, wider, and have bright yellow stripes. The variegated leaves will need at least a medium light to keep the variegation bright.

CROWN
OF THORNS

BOTANICAL NAME: *Euphorbia milii*

Though this plant has many spines, it is not a cactus; it's a succulent member of the spurge family. The spines may be hard to see as they are hidden by many oblong leaves. The common name comes from the fanciful idea that the crown of thorns Jesus wore may have been made out of these plants.

The crown of thorns has come a long way in the last few years with many new hybrids. There are Thai hybrids that have bracts (modified leaves) and flowers that resemble hydrangea heads and are quite large. The colors of the bracts, formerly only red, now come in myriad colors, including pink, green, bicolor, splotched, and more. These cousins of poinsettias also have tiny flowers surrounded by colorful bracts that are much larger than the actual flowers. Take care when handling this plant, not only because of the many spines, but because the plant has a white sap that can be irritating. Do not get it in your mouth or eyes.

LIGHT PREFERENCE: Give these plants as much light as you can. A south or west window would be best.

WATERING: Do not let these succulents completely dry out. If allowed to dry out, the leaves will yellow and fall off. If that happens, as soon as water is applied, they should regrow leaves. Grow in a fast-draining potting medium.

FLOWER: As previously mentioned, the true flowers are very small but surrounded by colorful bracts ranging from yellow to pink, red, and more. Depending on the light, moisture, and warmth, these plants may bloom on and off all year.

SIZE: There are miniature plants that may only reach a few inches to plants that may reach over 3 feet (0.9 m) in the home setting.

PROPAGATION: Tip cuttings can be taken and placed in a moist potting medium.

CULTIVARS:

- **'NORTHERN LIGHTS'**—The variegated leaves of this cultivar make it a stand out. It still has the red bracts surrounding the flowers.

- **'PINK CADILLAC'**—The bright pink bracts surrounding the flowers stand out against the large, oblong, bright green leaves.

- **'LEMON DROP'**—A miniature plant with small yellow bracts perfect for small dish gardens.

- **'SPLENDENS'**—A miniature plant with small red bracts. Perfect for a fairy garden.

DEVIL'S BACKBONE, RICK RACK PLANT, RED BIRD FLOWER

BOTANICAL NAME: *Pedilanthus tithymaloides*

The stems of this plant are its main attraction. They zigzag back and forth like rickrack, thus the common name, adding to the beauty of this plant.

LIGHT PREFERENCE: Give your rick rack plant plenty of light to keep it compact. A south or west window would be best.

WATERING: This is a succulent and so should be watered when the top inch or two of potting medium is dry. Do not let it become too dry as it will drop leaves, leaving bare stems showing. Remember, though it is a succulent and more drought tolerant, water it so that water runs out of the bottom of the pot. Do not allow it to stand in water.

FLOWER: Small flowers are covered by bracts shaped like slippers and are borne on the tips of the plants, but most likely you won't see blooms in the home.

SIZE: These plants range from miniature version only 10 to 12 inches (25.4 to 30.5 cm) high to the larger versions that may exceed 3 feet (0.9 m) tall.

PROPAGATION: Take cuttings, let them callus for a day or more, then plant in a moist medium.

CULTIVARS:

• *PEDILANTHUS TITHYMALOIDES* 'Nana'— This miniature version of the larger plant does not have the zigzag in the stem and only grows 10 to 12 inches (25.4 to 30.5 cm) tall.

• *P. TITHYMALOIDES VARIEGATUS* (left)— The variegated form has green and white leaves with touches of pink.

• *P. TITHYMALOIDES* 'Splish Splash'—This cultivar has bright green leaves with splotches of dark green.

DRACAENA

BOTANICAL NAME: *Dracaena deremensis*

Dracaenas are some of the most popular and easiest houseplants to grow. They thrive in a medium to bright light but do quite well in low-light conditions. The hybrid 'Janet Craig' is most often used as a low-light plant in commercial settings, but is a nice houseplant for a low-light home setting as well. The fountain-like look of the dark green leaves makes a nice statement in a low-light corner or it can cover a bare spot that needs some life. The variegated varieties need a much brighter place to keep their color. The leaves get dusty quickly, so either give the plant a shower when necessary or wipe down the leaves often.

LIGHT PREFERENCE: As previously discussed, these plants are quite tolerant of low-light levels, but prefer a medium light to really thrive.

WATERING: The dracaenas as a group do not like to be overly wet, but evenly moist. They are sensitive to fluoride in tap water, so if your metropolitan water has this chemical added, using rainwater or bottled water will prevent the plant tips from browning.

FLOWER: A stem of white flowers can sprout from among the leaves but most often will not be seen in the home setting.

SIZE: These plants can reach large proportions, but most likely won't grow to more than 10 feet (3 m) in your home, and that after many years. To keep it smaller, you can cut the tops off, rooting them in the same pot or starting them in another container.

PROPAGATION: Propagate by taking cuttings and rooting them in moist potting medium. This is the easiest method, but air layering (see page 25) could be used as well.

CULTIVARS:

• **'JANET CRAIG COMPACTA'**—This small version of Janet Craig has leaves usually not more than 5 to 6 inches (12.7 to 15.2 cm) long, and the growth is very compact with the individual stems of leaves only reaching 10 inches (25.4 cm) across. This plant is quite slow growing.

• **'DORADO'**—A dark green cultivar with dark green leaves and thin chartreuse edges.

• **'LEMON LIME'** (above)—Green leaves with yellow edges and a white strip down the middle. Beautiful variegated form.

• **'LEMON SURPRISE'**—With similar variegation to 'Lemon Lime' except with a slight twist in the leaves for added interest.

• **'LIMELIGHT'**—A completely bright chartreuse color that adds a bright accent to any area.

• **'RIKKI'**—These thinner than most, dark green leaves have a light green stripe down the middle.

• **'WARNECKII'**—This older variety sports green leaves with stripes of darker green and white.

DRAGON TREE

BOTANICAL NAME: *Dracaena marginata*

These strappy-leaved houseplants are very popular with humans and, unfortunately, kitties enjoy nibbling on them as well; the leaves must remind them of large grass blades. The plants can become very picturesque with age, as their trunks can become twisted and contorted. The stems, though uniquely shaped, will have tufts of foliage at the ends only. If they become too large for the house, they can be trimmed back and the cut ends rooted. It will take years for a small plant to become overly large.

LIGHT PREFERENCE: Though these plants can tolerate low-light levels, they prefer a medium to bright light. If the plant is variegated, which they quite often are, they will need a more intense light to keep the color.

WATERING: Keep the medium evenly moist during the growing season, but drier during the darker, cooler winter months. If this plant is overwatered, the canes will rot.

FLOWER: It does produce fragrant white flowers, but likely not in the home setting.

SIZE: When mature, they may reach upward of 10 feet (3 m).

PROPAGATION: The stem tips can be clipped off and placed in a moist potting media to root. The stem that has had the top cut off will sprout new growth with time. This works well when the plant has become too tall. The top can be cut back drastically and the resprouting cane will start out shorter. Air layering would work as well, but would be a much slower process. Stem cuttings (without foliage) can also be taken and planted; make sure the bottom end of the cane is in the potting medium.

CULTIVARS:

- **'COLORAMA'**—This newer cultivar appears to be a purely bright pink plant when in reality it is variegated with white and green. The color is stunning and will need a very bright light to keep the striking color bright.

- **'TRICOLOR'**—This older but still beautiful cultivar has three colors in its leaves, including green, white, and dark pink/red.

DUMB CANE

BOTANICAL NAME: *Dieffenbachia seguine*

The main feature of this plant is the attractive foliage. The common name comes from the fact that the plant sap contains calcium oxalate crystals that can burn the mouth and throat and may cause a temporary paralysis of the vocal chords. Keep this plant away from children and pets. The large leaves boast splotches and patches of darker green or white, making it a beautiful foliage plant.

LIGHT PREFERENCE: Place in a medium to bright light such as in an east or west window.

WATERING: Keep this plant evenly moist and raise the humidity by placing the container on a pebble tray.

FLOWER: White flowers followed by red berries will most likely not appear on plants in a home setting.

SIZE: There are many cultivars ranging from under 1 foot (0.3 m) tall to 4 to 5 feet (1.2 to 1.5 m) tall.

PROPAGATION: Cut the top few inches off a stem and root in a moist medium. The stems or canes can be cut into pieces, each with a node, and laid horizontally on a moist medium to root.

CULTIVARS: There are too many to list, but here are a few striking varieties to look for:

• **'CAMILLE'**—A bright chartreuse leaf with dark green edges.

• **'CAMOUFLAGE'**—A bright chartreuse leaf with splotches of dark green scattered over the leaf.

• **'STERLING'**—A medium-size plant with a dark green leaf that has a chartreuse green midrib and veins running through it.

• **'TROPIC SNOW'**—This large variety can grow to 5 feet (1.5 m) or more in height and has a bright green leaf with a yellow middle feathering into the green edges.

• **'TROPIC HONEY'**—This large variety has all yellow leaves with a thick, dark green edge.

DWARF
ALOES

BOTANICAL NAME: *Aloe* sp.

These small cultivars are newer and have taken the succulent world by storm. They are small, colorful, and not too spiky. They stay under 5 inches (12.7 cm) and form many offsets, making them easy to propagate and share. They are often sold in the spring at garden centers for combination dish gardens. A few cultivars are mentioned here, but there are numerous others.

LIGHT PREFERENCE: Give these plants as much light as you can to keep them compact and colorful. If they have lots of light, they will produce more offsets.

WATERING: Water thoroughly and then allow the potting medium to dry out a bit so as not to rot them. If they become too dry, the plant edges will curl.

FLOWER: These plants will have colorful flowers, usually in the orange range, but most likely will not bloom in the house.

SIZE: Small rosettes usually a few inches tall and wide.

PROPAGATION: Separate the offsets from the parent and pot up individually.

CULTIVARS:

- **'BLIZZARD'**—A version that has so many white tubercles on the green leaves, they are almost all white.

- **'DORAN BLACK'**—A dark chocolate-colored leaf covered with white spots.

- **'PINK BLUSH'**—Green leaves covered with oblong tubercles with pink edges.

DYCKIA BROMELIAD

As spiny as the edges of the leaves of dyckia are, one could mistake it as being related to the cactus family. It is actually related to the air plants or tillandsias, and the fruit-bearing pineapple plant. They aren't epiphytes as the tillandsias are, though, but terrestrial, like the pineapple plant, growing primarily on the ground. When handling these plants, wear gloves, as the spines can be painful. They are an unusual plant with many colorful varieties.

LIGHT PREFERENCE: Dyckias prefer full sun, so a south window is best in the home setting.

WATERING: Dyckias need to be in a well-drained potting medium. Do not overwater; be especially careful of this in the lower-light times of the year.

FLOWER: They produce orange or yellow flowers, pollinated by hummingbirds in their native habitat. Flowers will most likely not appear in the home setting unless the light is exceptionally high.

SIZE: They range in size from 6 inches to 3 feet (15.2 to 91.4 cm) across and range from a few inches to a foot or taller.

PROPAGATION: These plants multiply by offsets at the base of the parent plant. When they are a good size, they can be separated and potted up individually. This process will require gloves to protect hands from the spines on the leaves.

CULTIVARS:

- **'BRITTLE STAR'**—This very attractive plant is grayish white with a burgundy midrib.

- **'CHERRY COLA'**—This newer hybrid has shiny dark red leaves.

- **'NAKED LADY'**—The name is as it implies. The green leaves have no spines at all.

EUPHORBIA DECARYI VAR. DECARYI

The leaves on this small, spreading succulent have edges that resemble fluted piecrusts. The diminutive size of this small Madagascar species makes it perfect for a bright windowsill. Tiny flowers form at the ends of the stems and are a peachy color. It is a must for a collector of succulents and perfect for miniature gardens.

LIGHT PREFERENCE: Place these small plants on a south or west windowsill.

WATERING: This plant can take drier conditions, but will drop leaves if dried out too much.

FLOWER: The flower are very small, approximately ¼-inch (0.6 cm) wide. The two bracts surrounding the flowers overlap and resemble a small bell, peach in color.

SIZE: These small spreading plants are slow growers and may never need a pot larger than 3 inches (7.6 cm). They will only be a few inches high.

PROPAGATION: Take stem cuttings, allow the ends to dry or callus, and plant in a moist potting medium.

FAIRY
WASHBOARD

SIZE: The small rosette of leaves will be approximately 2 inches (5.1 cm) tall and not more than 4 inches (10.2 cm) wide.

PROPAGATION: Remove offsets from the base of the plant and pot up individually.

CULTIVARS: A variegated form of this plant is worth the search, as it is beautiful, but it is not easy to find and may be costly.

•*HAWORTHIA LIMIFOLIA* var. *stricta*—The ridges on this variety are white.

BOTANICAL NAME: *Haworthia limifolia*

Haworthias are the perfect succulents for our homes, as they need less light than most succulents, which need full sun. The flower grows in a small rosette, and each leaf has ridges protruding from the surface, giving it its common name. This small succulent rarely reaches more than 4 inches (10.2 cm) across, making it ideal for an indoor fairy garden, especially given its name.

LIGHT PREFERENCE: Place this succulent in medium to bright light. Do not give it the full sun other succulents prefer, as it will turn to burgundy and may sunburn.

WATERING: These succulents need the potting medium to become almost completely dry before watering again, especially if they are growing in a lower light level.

FLOWER: The flower stalk will appear from the center of the rosette and may extend over 2 feet (0.6 m) long with small, white, trumpet-shaped flowers.

FIRE FLASH
SPIDER PLANT

BOTANICAL NAME: *Chlorophytum amaniense* 'Fire Flash'

This colorful relative of the much-loved spider or airplane plant in no way resembles its cousin. Vibrant orange petioles hold up dark-green leaves, providing a beautiful contrast.

LIGHT PREFERENCE: To keep its bright orange color, it needs a medium-light situation as in an east window. In general, this is a houseplant that will thrive on less light rather than more, a trait it shares with the peace lily (or *spathiphyllum*). Too much light will cause the foliage to look bleached and pale.

WATERING: Keep the 'Fire Flash' evenly moist. It prefers water without fluoride as fluoride will burn the tips of the plants.

FLOWER: The white flowers, resembling those of the spider plant, appear on a short stalk that arises from the middle of the plant. If left on the plant, it will produce seedpods; when they open and fall into the container, they will sprout new babies.

PROPAGATION: Collect the seeds after blooming and sow in a moist medium, or wait for the seeds to sprout in the container and pot up the babies individually.

FLAME VIOLET

BOTANICAL NAME: *Episcia* sp.

The flame violet is so called for its bright red flowers and the fact that it is related to the African violet. They are both in the Gesneriad family. It is primarily grown for its colorful, vibrant foliage. These plants love warmth and humidity, making them perfect for terrarium culture. They grow an abundance of stolons or runners (like a strawberry plant), so they are well suited to a hanging basket, which is how they are usually offered for sale.

LIGHT PREFERENCE: It prefers a bright but indirect light. An east window is perfect, but it can also be grown under electric lights.

WATERING: Keep the episcia evenly moist and raise the humidity around the plant by placing the container on a pebble tray.

FLOWER: The tubular flowers may be white, yellow, lavender, pink, or red, depending on the variety.

SIZE: Whereas the plant is only a few inches tall, if left to spread, it can grow to 18 inches (45.7 cm) wide or more.

PROPAGATION: New episcia can be grown from the small plantlets at the end of the runners.

GASTERALOE 'LITTLE WARTY'

Gasteraloes are a cross between the genera gasteria and aloe. They form a rosette of stiff succulent leaves. The stripes of green and white and the warty texture make for an interesting succulent. Its ease of care and medium-light requirements add to the popularity of this plant.

LIGHT PREFERENCE: A bright to medium light, such as an east or west window is best.

WATERING: Plant this succulent in a fast-draining potting medium. It needs water when the medium is almost completely dry.

FLOWER: The flowers have the color of gasteria flowers, usually orange with green, but have the shape of the aloe flower, which is tubular. The little stomach shape apparent in the gasteria genus is not present on the gasteraloe.

SIZE: The plant will spread sideways as it multiplies by offsets. It will only reach 4 to 5 inches (10.2 to 12.7 cm) in height.

PROPAGATION: Separate the offsets from the parent plant, and pot them up individually.

GASTERIA BICOLOR VAR. *LILIPUTANA*

This tiny gasteria rarely gets taller than an inch or two, and it may never need a container larger than 3 to 4 (7.6 to 10.2 cm) inches around. It's a small succulent that can reside on a windowsill, but only needs medium light. It is perfect for an indoor fairy garden.

LIGHT PREFERENCE: The gasterias as a group really only need a medium light compared to most full-sun succulents. If it is a variegated plant, it will need a little more light to keep its variegation.

WATERING: As these are succulents, they need to be planted in a fast-draining potting medium and watered only when the medium is almost completely dry.

SIZE: This tiny variety is only an inch or two tall and can become 2 to 3 inches (5.1 to 7.6 cm) across as it produces many offsets.

PROPAGATION: Separate the offsets from the parent plant, and pot them up individually.

GOLDEN BARREL CACTUS

BOTANICAL NAME: *Echinocactus grusonii*

These iconic cacti are most often seen in conservatories and are endangered in their native Mexico, where they are said to naturally slant slightly to the south, like living compasses. The golden spines and globe shape of these plants make for a striking specimen and one well suited for full-sun areas. The spikes are plentiful so they must be handled with extreme care when moving or repotting. As the plant ages, it will become more oblong than round.

LIGHT PREFERENCE: In your home, give the barrel cactus as much light as possible. Close to an unobstructed south window would be best.

WATERING: In the house, don't let the medium completely dry out, especially in the summer when it is actively growing. In the winter, water should be applied sparingly, if at all. If it is in a cool room, do not water as it may rot the plant.

FLOWER: This plant produces yellow flowers, but most likely it will not bloom in the home environment.

SIZE: The barrel cactus may reach 1 to 3 feet (0.3 to 0.9 m) tall in the house.

PROPAGATION: These can be propagated from seeds.

GOLDFISH PLANT

BOTANICAL NAME: *Nematanthus gregarius*

The flowers of this vining plant resemble small orange fish. It is a cousin of African violets but tends to epiphytic in its natural habitat; it is most often sold in hanging baskets.

LIGHT PREFERENCE: To expect the cute, goldfish-like flowers to appear, a medium to bright light is needed. An east or west window is sufficient, or grow them under electric lights to ensure blooms.

WATERING: Keep this plant evenly moist, especially while blooming, to keep the flowers looking their best.

FLOWER: With the correct light, these plants could have flowers year-round.

SIZE: The goldfish plant is often offered as a hanging basket and is only a few inches high, but the stems may hang 12 to 15 inches (30.5 to 38.1 cm) down from the edge of the basket.

PROPAGATION: Take tip cuttings a few inches long and insert them into a moist potting medium.

CULTIVARS:

• **'BLACK GOLD'**—A cultivar with dark green, almost-burgundy foliage that makes the golden flowers more obvious.

• **'TROPICANA'**—The flowers of this cultivar have burgundy lines running through the orange flowers.

• **'VARIEGATA'**—The leaves are green and cream.

GRAPE IVY

BOTANICAL NAME: *Cissus rhombifolia* 'Ellen Danica'

A vining plant, grape ivy is a perfect plant for a trellis or hanging basket. It has dark green leaves that are separated into leaflets, which resemble small oak leaves rather than grape leaves. It's a robust plant that can cover a problem spot or a dark corner quickly.

LIGHT PREFERENCE: This is a versatile vine that can tolerate a low-light north window but prefers a medium light in an east or west window.

WATERING: Plant in a peat-based but well-drained medium, and keep the plant evenly moist. Do not allow it to stand in water, but if it dries out, it will drop leaves.

SIZE: This vine can reach lengths of 10 to 12 feet (3 to 3.7 m). Trim to keep it a more manageable size if needed.

PROPAGATION: Take tip cuttings and root in a moist potting medium.

HEARTLEAF PHILODENDRON

BOTANICAL NAME: *Philodendron hederaceum*

The heartleaf philodendron is undeniably the most loved houseplant of all time. The heart-shaped leaves and ease of care account for its popularity. Many a window has been framed by this endearing vine. The newer cultivars have kept its popularity high.

LIGHT PREFERENCE: This philodendron can survive in low light but will thrive in medium light, such as an east or west window.

WATERING: This is a forgiving plant if it dries out, but it prefers to be kept evenly moist. It does not want to be wet, though.

FLOWER: It is grown for its foliage.

SIZE: This trailing plant can get quite long, but it can be kept bushy by trimming some of the stems back to the soil line. New shoots will emerge.

PROPAGATION: Take stem tip cuttings and pot in a moist potting medium.

CULTIVARS:

• **'LEMON LIME'**—Bright green leaves.

• **'BRASIL'**—Dark green leaves with bright green stripes.

• *PHILODENDRON BRANDTIANUM*—Gray leaves with dark green veins.

HENS AND CHICKS

BOTANICAL NAME: *Echeveria* sp.

Echeverias are tropical hens and chicks and are quite often mistaken for sempervivums, their hardy northern look-alikes. On the other hand, they like to be kept warm and given plenty of light. If exposed to freezing temperatures, they may die. If you have a high-light window, these would be perfect. These succulents come in many different forms and colors.

LIGHT PREFERENCE: Choose the brightest spot in the house, such as a south-facing windowsill. If in too low a light, these succulents will stretch for the light. They may still stretch even in an unobstructed south window, so in winter benefit from being grown under electric lights.

WATERING: These succulents need a fast-draining potting medium. Water thoroughly, then let the medium almost dry out before watering again. In the winter, wait longer to water than you did in the growing season.

FLOWER: The flowers of echeverias are usually orange or yellow and are held on arching stems about 1 foot (0.3 m) above the foliage.

SIZE: There are small varieties that are inches across to large varieties that can be 2 feet (0.6 m) across.

PROPAGATION: Echeverias make offsets which can be separated and potted up individually. Echeverias can also be propagated by individual leaves. Pull a leaf off, let the end callus over, and then lay on top of a moist medium. Small plantlets will form at the end of the leaf. The whole plant can be cut off its stem and laid onto of a container of potting medium, and it will form roots. The naked stem may sprout new plantlets that can also be removed and potted.

CULTIVARS: There are so many cultivars to choose from. Here are just a few:

• **'BLACK PRINCE'**—This is a cultivar with dark burgundy leaves.

• **'PERLE VON NURNBERG'**—A purplish-gray sheen is the main feature of this cultivar.

• **'TOPSY TURVY'**—The gray color of this popular cultivar isn't too memorable, but the shape of the leaves is. They turn up at the ends and come to a point.

• *ECHEVERIA SHAVIANA* **'ROSEA'**—This cultivar has ruffled edges on a blue-colored plant with purple shading. A showstopper!

JEWEL ORCHID

BOTANICAL NAME: *Ludisia discolor*

This terrestrial orchid is grown for its beautiful foliage more than for its spikes of white flowers. The burgundy foliage has iridescent peach stripes. This is an extremely easy orchid to grow in potting medium and achieve bloom in a medium-light window. These plants can become leggy as they get older. After rooting the tip cuttings, plant them back in the pot to help the plant stay fuller and more attractive.

LIGHT PREFERENCE: These orchids are found in shady places in their native habitat, so they are perfect for our homes. They do need a bright light to bloom, though, so give them a medium light, such as an east window. Turn your plant regularly to promote flowering on the entire plant.

WATERING: Keep the medium evenly moist and plant in a heavy, peat-based potting medium.

FLOWER: The small flowers are white and appear on flower stems that rise above the foliage approximately 12 inches (30.5 cm).

SIZE: The foliage is only a few inches high but the stems do extend over the edge of the pot and hang down approximately 8 to 10 inches (20.3 to 25.4 cm). These plants would make an excellent hanging basket.

PROPAGATION: Tip cuttings are easily rooted in moist potting medium. The plant could also be cut apart and pieces potted up individually.

JUNGLE FLAME, JUNGLE GERANIUM

BOTANICAL NAME: *Ixora* sp.

The ixora is most often used as a summer bedding plant or in a summer container in the north. In the south, it is used for hedges. In the house, it is a medium-size houseplant that needs bright light to bloom. If it does not receive enough light to bloom, its bright green leathery leaves still make for a nice foliage plant, with the new growth starting out as a burnt orange color.

LIGHT PREFERENCE: Find a place with bright light to place this plant. A south or west window will work well to promote flowering.

WATERING: Humidity and warmth are necessary with an evenly moist potting medium. If the plant dries out, it may drop leaves.

SIZE: This is a 4- to 6-foot (1.2 to 1.8 m) plant in nature, but will probably grow less than 2 feet (0.6 m) tall in your home. Trim to keep the growth in check and keep the plant full.

PROPAGATION: Cuttings can be taken, but high humidity and bottom heat may be necessary to root.

LIFESAVER PLANT

BOTANICAL NAME: *Huernia zebrina*

A unique flower gives rise to the name lifesaver plant. The center of the flower does look like a shiny, burgundy inner tube or lifesaver. It's a succulent, easy to grow and bloom in a bright light.

LIGHT PREFERENCE: A south or west window will provide enough light to get this show-stopping plant to bloom.

WATERING: Keep this succulent on the dry side but do not let it dry out completely, especially when in flower.

FLOWER: The unassuming plant doesn't wow, but the unique flower will. It's shaped like a burgundy, rubber lifesaver with burgundy-speckled, cream-colored triangular petals surrounding it. The flower is approximately 1 inch (2.5 cm) across.

SIZE: This small, 3- to 4-inch (7.6 to 10.2 cm) succulent can spread out as wide as the container it is growing in. A short, wide container, such as a bulb pan, with drainage would be perfect.

PROPAGATION: Stem cuttings will root in a moist potting medium after the cuttings are allowed to callus over.

LIPSTICK PLANT

BOTANICAL NAME: *Aeschynanthus radicans*

The lipstick plant is so named for the beautiful, bright reddish-orange flowers that appear as if they are rising out of a tube of lipstick. Usually sold as hanging baskets, these plants are cousins of African violets in the Gesneriad family and like similar growing conditions.

LIGHT PREFERENCE: Grow in an east or west window or under electric lights for the most blooms. Turn the plant often if growing in a window to ensure equal blooms on all sides.

WATERING: Keep the plant evenly moist. These plants are quite often grown in a mix with a large amount of peat, so if the plant is allowed to dry out, it is hard to re-wet the medium. To prevent rot, do not let the plant stand in water.

FLOWER: The red flowers emerge from calyxes (sepals of a flower), giving the appearance of a lipstick emerging from its container.

SIZE: This vine is 12 to 24 inches (30.5 to 61 cm) long.

PROPAGATION: Take tip cuttings and pot in a moist potting medium.

CULTIVARS:

- **'TANGERINE'**—Dark green foliage with yellow flowers.

- **'VARIEGATA'**—White variegation in the leaves with red-orange flowers.

- **'RASTA'**—The curled foliage gives this cultivar its interest.

LUCKY BAMBOO

BOTANICAL NAME: *Dracaena sanderiana*

Lucky bamboo, which is not a bamboo at all, has been popular since it first came to the market in the late 1990s. It is said to bring luck and is used extensively in feng shui. If the stem curls, it has been trained that way by using phototropism to make the plant grow and turn toward light. This is an easy plant to grow in water only, which is how it is often offered for sale.

LIGHT PREFERENCE: Place this plant in bright light. Full sun would be too much for it, so place it in an east window or back a few feet from a south or west window.

WATERING: This plant is most often grown exclusively in water, but it can be grown in a potting medium as well. Dracaenas do not like the chemicals in tap water, so use rain water or distilled water, if possible. Change the water at least one to two times per month, and keep the water at the same level all the time. If grown in soil, keep it evenly moist.

FLOWER: It's not likely to flower in the home.

SIZE: These canes can be only an inch tall to many feet tall. They can be kept trimmed.

PROPAGATION: Cuttings can be taken and rooted in moist potting medium or placed in water to grow roots. If you cut the top of the cane off, new sprouts will emerge lower on the cane. The cane piece that has been cut off, if it still has green leaves attached, can be placed in water to grow new roots.

MADAGASCAR PALM

BOTANICAL NAME: *Pachypodium lamerei*

The Madagascar palm is a succulent with spines. The leaves mostly grow on the top of the stem, giving it a palm-like look. The stem has a silver color, further adding to its beauty.

LIGHT PREFERENCE: Give this plant as much light as possible. It will stretch if not given enough light.

WATERING: Plant in a fast-draining potting medium and, after watering thoroughly, let the medium dry down quite a bit before watering again. Overwatering or allowing the plant to stand in water will rot it.

FLOWER: It does produce white flowers at the top of the plant, but most likely will not flower in the home setting.

SIZE: It could reach 18 to 20 feet (5.1 to 6.1 m) in its natural habitat, but usually only reaches less than 6 feet (1.8 m) in the home.

PROPAGATION: Take a cutting and allow it to callus over before planting in a moist potting medium.

MINI
MONSTERA VINE

BOTANICAL NAME: *Rhaphidophora tetrasperma*

This vining plant resembles (and is related to) the Swiss cheese plant *Monstera deliciosa*, but the leaves will only ever achieve a size of 6 inches (15.2 cm). It's easy to grow and can tolerate low light.

LIGHT PREFERENCE: It would like a medium light, but can tolerate low light. A north, east, or west window would work well. No direct sun is needed, as too much light can cause the leaves to bleach.

WATERING: Keep the potting medium evenly moist. If the plant is in low light, it will need less water.

FLOWER: It most likely will not flower in the home.

SIZE: This vine can grow 6 to 10 feet (1.8 to 3 m) in length.

PROPAGATION: Stem cuttings can be rooted in a moist potting medium.

MINI
UMBRELLA TREE

BOTANICAL NAME: *Schefflera arboricola*

This plant is the mini version of the umbrella tree, *Schefflera actinophylla*. Seven to nine leaflets arranged in a whorl on short stems cover this small shrub-like plant. The leaves are bright green, and most often the variegated versions are the ones offered for sale.

LIGHT PREFERENCE: Give it a medium to bright light. The variegated versions need more light than the all-green ones.

WATERING: Water thoroughly and allow the medium to dry down a bit before watering again. It is easy to rot this plant, so keeping it on the drier side is better than keeping it wet. Keep it drier in the winter when the light levels are lower.

FLOWER: It does have tiny red flowers but most likely will not produce them in the house.

SIZE: In its native habitat, this plant can be 10 to 25 feet (3 to 7.6 m) tall, but in the home it may be 3 to 6 feet (0.9 to 1.8 m) tall.

PROPAGATION: Root the tip cuttings in a moist potting medium.

CULTIVARS:

- **'DAZZLE'**—This variety is variegated with white.

- **'GOLD CAPELLA'**—This variety is variegated with yellow.

MISTLETOE CACTUS

BOTANICAL NAME: *Rhipsalis*

Called the mistletoe cactus for its appearance and its habit of hanging out in trees, this plant grows as an epiphyte. It is a cactus, but a tropical rainforest one, not the typical desert variety. You won't notice any spines, but a few do have bristles. The small cream to white flowers turn into white berries, furthering the mistletoe resemblance. They have a tendency to have a weeping form and so are most often sold in hanging baskets.

LIGHT PREFERENCE: This is a plant that can take less light then most cacti. A bright light and high humidity, which mimic their natural habitat, is best. Hang in a south or west window for the best results.

WATERING: Water thoroughly and then allow the plant to dry a bit before watering again. Too much water will rot this plant, however, if underwatered, pieces of the plants will begin to fall off.

FLOWER: Small white, cream, or yellow flowers may appear on this plant if it is exposed to enough light.

SIZE: Whether in a regular pot or a hanging basket, the branches may cascade a foot (0.3 m) or more over the sides of the container.

PROPAGATION: Cut off segments of the stems and allow the ends to callus over, then plant them in a moist potting medium.

MONEY TREE, GUIANA CHESTNUT

BOTANICAL NAME: *Pachira aquatica*

This popular plant has taken the last decade by storm. The feng shui movement brought pachira to the forefront, as it is purported to bring good luck. The plant is usually sold with a braided trunk and the five to seven bright green leaflets that make up one leaf are unusual and beautiful. It is often sold as a bonsai as well. Its ease of care and low-light tolerance also add to the popularity. There is some confusion whether the plant most often sold is *Pachira aquatic* or *P. glabra*, but since the only way to tell the difference is by seeing the flower, we probably won't know because it is unlikely to flower in our homes.

LIGHT PREFERENCE: A medium to bright light is best, such as that offered by an east or west window.

WATERING: This plant grows in water in its native habitat, but as a houseplant, do not leave it standing in water. Keep the soil evenly moist.

FLOWER: Large, yellowish-white flowers have five recurving petals surrounding a shaving brush—like agroup of stamens with red tips. Each flower turns into a large woody pod, encasing a nut that is said to taste like a peanut. The flowers most likely will not appear in the home situation.

SIZE: In nature, this plant becomes a 50- to 60-foot (15.2 to 18.3 m) tree, but can be kept to 6 to 8 feet (1.8 to 2.4 m) in your home. Do not up-pot the tree when it gets to the size you would like to keep it. Instead, root prune it, trim the top, and return it to the same size container.

PROPAGATION: Take tip cuttings and root them in a moist potting medium.

MOSES IN THE CRADLE, OYSTER PLANT

BOTANICAL NAME: *Rhoeo spathacea*

The two bracts that surround the small white flower resemble shells, thus the common name of oyster plant. Of course, the white flower cradled down in the bracts brings to mind Moses floating down the river in his basket. This plant, used for a groundcover in the south, makes a good low- to medium-light houseplant. The upward pointing leaves allow the purple undersides to show. The tops of the leaves are dark green.

LIGHT PREFERENCE: If it is not a variegated cultivar, this plant can take a low to medium light, such as a north or east window. If it has variegation, a medium to bright light is recommended, such as an east or west window.

WATERING: Keep this plant evenly moist, making sure not to overwater, as it can easily rot. It would be better to err on the side of dry rather than wet. It will appreciate a higher humidity to ensure the tips do not turn brown.

FLOWER: A small white flower, surrounded by two bracts deep in the leaves of the plant, is apparent only when you think to look for it.

SIZE: This plant grows to 1 to 1½ feet (0.3 to 0.5 m) tall.

PROPAGATION: Remove offsets and pot them up separately.

CULTIVARS:

- **'TRICOLOR'** (below)—This newer, popular cultivar is bright green with white and pink stripes; the undersides of the leaves are bright pink.

- **'VITTATA'**—An older cultivar that has yellow stripes on the green tops of the leaves; this plant boasts purple undersides.

MOTH ORCHID

BOTANICAL NAME: *Phalaenopsis*

Moth orchids were once only attainable to the wealthy. Tissue culture has made this gorgeous plant available to almost everyone. The cultivars and flower colors are endless and more are being hybridized every day. The only color they don't come in is blue. If you see the blue ones for sale, they have been sprayed with vegetable dye and succeeding generations of flowers will be snow white. The best part is how easy they are to bring into bloom again.

LIGHT PREFERENCE: Moth orchids need a medium to bright light to produce flowers. An east or west window is best.

WATERING: Take your plant to the sink, and remove it from the decorative pot or sleeve. Run water through the actual pot, and then allow it to drain. Return to the decorative pot and to the spot it was growing. If water gets in the middle of the leaves, make sure to blot it out with a paper towel, as standing water may rot the plant.

FLOWER: Once the flower stalk has appeared, the plant can be moved to any spot, because they don't need the same light to continue to bloom. The flowers can last for months as long as the plant isn't allowed to dry out or stand in water. When the flowers fade, cut off the stem at the base to allow the plant to put all its energy into growing and making a bigger and better display of flowers the next year. If you cut the stem above the second node (swollen area on the stem), it may send out another display of flowers.

SIZE: The plant itself is usually 6 to 8 inches (15.2 to 20.3 cm) tall and approximately 12 inches (30.5 cm) wide. The flower stems will rise above the plants 24 to 30 inches (61 to 76.2 cm). There are also miniature moth orchids only a few inches high.

PROPAGATION: Occasionally, small plantlets called *keikis* appear on the flower stem at the nodes. Care for the plant as usual, allowing the small plantlets to grow larger. When they have roots a few inches long, cut from the parent and pot individually.

NEOPORTERIA NIDUS

This is a striking cactus with dark spines that have a white, woolly covering that protects it from sunburn and keeps it cooler in its native desert habitat. The more sun you give this plant, the woolier it will become. Since this is the main attraction of this cactus, give it a lot of sun! Plant in a coarse, well-drained potting medium to give it plenty of good drainage.

LIGHT PREFERENCE: A south or west windowsill will give it the sun it needs.

WATERING: Do not overwater this plant as it may lead to root rot and plant collapse. If it is on a windowsill that gets cold, it will probably not need any water until the days lengthen and the sill warms up.

FLOWER: A group of hot pink, trumpet-shaped, shaggy flowers will protrude out of the top of the plant with enough sun.

SIZE: This small, globose cactus reaches 4 to 6 inches (10.2 to 15.2 cm) tall.

PROPAGATION: This plant is started from seed as it seldom produces offsets.

NEOREGELIA
CAROLINAE

A member of the *bromeliad* family, which includes the pineapple, neoregelias are some of the most colorful and easy houseplants. Do not give these plants a fertilizer containing a large amount of nitrogen, as it will turn the colorful leaves green. These plants are usually sold in a container with potting medium, but they are quite often epiphytes in their native habitat.

LIGHT PREFERENCE: A medium to bright light, such as an east or west window, will keep the neoregelia colorful and growing.

WATERING: The shape of this plant makes a natural urn or vase in the center of the plant, and this needs to be kept filled with fresh water. When adding water, fill the urn to overflowing so that some spills into the potting medium. The potting mix does not need more water than that, as the roots merely anchor the plant. Empty the vase completely and refill often.

FLOWER: The flowers bloom down in the vase and are pretty, but not obvious. The plant is grown for its beautiful foliage.

SIZE: Neoregelias range from a few inches high to a few feet high and wide, depending on the cultivar.

PROPAGATION: Once these plants flower, the parent plant will gradually die. Before it dies, small plantlets, called offsets or sometimes "pups," come up at the base of the parent. When these have reached one-third to one-half the size of the parent, they can be potted up individually.

CULTIVARS:

• **'FIREBALL'**—This smaller plant can form a very large clump of fiery red leaves. If the offsets are not removed and are allowed to stay attached to each other, the result is a large clump that is quite striking.

• **'COTTON CANDY'**—The hot pink center of this plant brings to mind spun cotton candy.

• **'DEVROE'**—As if the variegated leaves weren't enough, the fireball red center makes it a showstopper.

• **'FRANCA'**—Yellow edges on a green leaf with a hot pink center make for a beautiful plant.

• **'INFERNO'**—This almost-white plant has green stripes with just a touch of red in the center.

OLD MAN
OF THE ANDES

BOTANICAL NAME: *Oreocereus celsianus*

The white furry covering of this cactus gives it the common name, along with the fact that it grows high in the Andes Mountains of South America. Its white covering is grown to protect it from sunburn. Do not let the cute woolly covering fool you, as it is very spiny underneath. If the "fur" becomes dusty or dirty, it can be washed on a warm day in a place with good air circulation to completely dry it out.

LIGHT PREFERENCE: In the home, it prefers bright light from a south or west windowsill.

WATERING: These plants need a fast-draining coarse mix to prevent root rot. Water very sparingly, as these plants rot easily. They do not like high or low temperatures. The more sun they have, the denser the white hair becomes. Try not to water on an overcast day or a cold winter day.

FLOWER: It can produce tubular red flowers in the spring, but will likely not do that in our homes.

SIZE: These plants can reach heights of 10 feet (3 m) in the mountains where they reside naturally. They grow slowly and may reach 1 to 2 feet (0.3 to 0.6 m) or more in the house.

PROPAGATION: Sow seed to propagate.

ORCHID CACTUS

BOTANICAL NAME: *Epiphyllum*

These are epiphytic rainforest cacti native to Central America, not related to orchids at all but more akin to what we call Christmas cactus. When they are blooming, there is nothing more beautiful! The large flowers come in myriad colors and are produced on the tips of the flattened stems.

LIGHT PREFERENCE: A sunny window, such as a south or west window, will promote flowering. However, they do not want to be in hot, direct sun. As they grow in trees in their native setting, they receive some dappled shade from the branches of the trees.

WATERING: Keep the potting medium evenly moist but never sitting in water. Water when the soil is dry about an inch or two deep. Cut back on watering in the winter when it is cooler and the light levels are low.

FLOWER: The flowers come in many colors and may be 10 to 12 inches (25.4 to 30.5 cm) wide and more. The original colors were white and yellow with some reds. Now, through hybridization, there are many beautiful colors available.

SIZE: These clambering plants may need a large hanging basket or a trellis to hold up their many stems. They can be kept trimmed and the cuttings used for new plants.

PROPAGATION: Allow leaf cuttings to dry for a week or more and then start in a moist potting medium. Roots should form in a few weeks.

OX-TONGUE

FLOWER: Most are orange with a green tip and hang from 2- to 3-foot-long (0.6 to 0.9 m) stems.

SIZE: Gasterias can range from a little over 1 inch (2.5 cm) high to more than 2 feet (0.6 m) tall.

PROPAGATION: They make quite a large number of offsets; these can be removed and potted up individually. They also can be started from seed. Single leaves can be removed, allowed to dry for a few weeks, and planted in a moist potting mix. Or they can be laid horizontally on the medium, and they will grow babies and roots from the cut end in a few months.

BOTANICAL NAME: *Gasteria carinata* var. *verrucosa*

Ox-tongue leaves are said by some to resemble a tongue. They do have a rounded tip and tubercles (small round protuberances) scattered over the leaves. They are easy to grow and they can be placed in lower light and still do well. The gasteria name comes from their flowers, which resemble the shape of a stomach. The plant will easily produce flowers on a west windowsill. This particular plant is dark green with white tubercles all over the leaves.

LIGHT PREFERENCE: Gasterias can thrive on a west or east windowsill and, in fact, could be placed a few feet from a south window and do well.

WATERING: These fleshy succulents should be planted in a fast-draining medium and never be allowed to stand in water. Keep drier in the winter when the light levels are lower.

PARALLEL PEPEROMIA, RADIATOR PLANT

BOTANICAL NAME: *Peperomia puteolata*

The parallel peperomia, though not technically a vine, does become a weeping plant with age and may be found for sale in a hanging basket. The leaves are whorled around the red stem in groupings of three to five and are heavily veined, with the veins running parallel to the edge of the leaves, thus the common name. This family of plants is quite easy to grow, as long as you do not overwater, as most are quite succulent whether in their leaves or their stems.

LIGHT PREFERENCE: Give this plant a medium-light situation, such as an east or west window.

WATERING: Plant in a well-drained potting medium and keep it evenly moist, but not wet.

SIZE: It can become up to 15 inches (38.1 cm) long.

PROPAGATION: Propagate from tip cuttings rooted in a moist potting medium.

PARTRIDGE BREAST ALOE, TIGER ALOE

BOTANICAL NAME: *Aloe variegata*

A popular, easy-to-find succulent, this aloe owes its name to the markings on the leaves, which resemble a partridge breast or a tiger's stripes. It is easy to grow on a bright windowsill as a 10- to 12-inch-tall (25.4 to 30.5 cm) plant, also contributing to its popularity.

LIGHT PREFERENCE: A bright light is best for this succulent, and if the light is high enough, it may flower.

WATERING: As this is a succulent, be light-handed with watering.

FLOWER: The flowers are orange red and appear on short stems. This may not occur in the home environment but may with enough light.

SIZE: A 10- to 12-inch-tall (25.4 to 30.5 cm) plant.

PROPAGATION: The plant sends out offsets from the base that can be removed and potted up separately.

PEACE LILY

BOTANICAL NAME: *Spathiphyllum*

Not a true lily, but instead related to the aglaonema, philodendron, and dieffenbachia, which are all aroids. These popular plants are easy to care for and forgiving of being allowed to wilt from underwatering. The white flowers appear with a medium light, which the plant prefers. The beautiful, shiny dark green leaves make it more attractive.

LIGHT PREFERENCE: The peace lily can tolerate a medium to low light, but flowers may not appear in less than a medium light. An east or north window would work well, but the east window will produce flowers while the north may not. It will flower 5 to 6 feet (1.5 to 1.8 m) away from a west window.

WATERING: This plant does not like to dry out, so keep it evenly moist. It will wilt from underwatering and come back quite well as soon as water is added to the medium. Some use the wilting as a visual indicator to water. Yet, if that happens often, it can result in leaves dying back from the tips. It is better to check it often and keep it moist.

FLOWER: The large, white, flag-like appendage of the peace lily is actually a spathe. The white upright cylinder that appears in the middle of the spathe is the spadix, and it is covered with tiny flowers. Pollen falls from them and can be seen on the leaves. Quite often in commercial settings, the spadix is removed to keep the leaves clean and pollen free.

SIZE: Peace lilies have many cultivars ranging from 1 foot (0.3 m) tall to over 4 feet (1.2 m) tall.

PROPAGATION: The peace lily is a multiple crown plant. The easy way to propagate it is to just separate the crowns and plant them up individually.

CULTIVARS:

- **'DOMINO'**—A variegated form that has white markings on the puckered leaves.

PERUVIAN OLD LADY CACTUS

FLOWER: It produces white flowers, but it is very unlikely in your home.

SIZE: It can reach up to 7 feet (2.1 m) tall in its native habitat, but in a home, it may reach 10 inches (25.4 cm).

PROPAGATION: This may be propagated from seed.

BOTANICAL NAME: *Espostoa melanostele*

This mountain-dwelling cactus grows white "hair" to protect itself from the intense sun it encounters in its native habitat. To make sure there is plenty of the white hair on your specimen, place it in as much sun as possible. Don't let the furry look of this plant fool you. There are plenty of sharp spines under there. Overwatering this cactus is its biggest killer.

LIGHT PREFERENCE: A bright light is a must for this light-loving cactus. A south or west windowsill would be the best spot for it.

WATERING: This cactus needs a light hand with the watering can. This is especially important in the winter when light levels are low and it is cold on the windowsill.

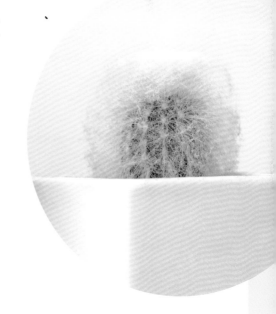

PHILODENDRON 'MOONLIGHT'

The bright chartreuse of this plant's leaves glows in a medium- to low-light spot in the home. This self-heading philodendron does not vine, so stays a reasonable size for the home situation. The large leaves start out a bright yellow, but fade to a darker green on the older leaves at the bottom of the plant.

LIGHT PREFERENCE: A medium light ensures you will have bright yellow leaves and good growth. An east or west window would be best. If it receives too much light, the leaves will bleach out and not have the best color.

WATERING: Philodendrons like to be evenly moist, neither too wet nor too dry.

FLOWER: Philodendrons produce a finger-like spadix surrounded by a spathe, but most likely will not bloom in the home.

SIZE: They may grow up to 2 feet (0.6 m) or more and equally that wide.

PROPAGATION: Take stem cuttings, and start in a moist potting medium.

CULTIVARS: Other colors have been hybridized and include orange and variegated leaves.

• **'PRINCE OF ORANGE'**—A hybrid with dark, rust-colored new growth and medium-green older leaves.

• **'AUTUMN'**—The new growth on this plant is a dark russet color that fades to a green.

• **'PINK PRINCESS'**—A newer variety with dark burgundy leaves splashed with bright pink splotches. This plant will vine and can be grown on a pole.

PINK BUTTERFLIES

BOTANICAL NAME: *Kalanchoe delagoensis* ×
daigremontiana 'Pink Butterflies'

This unique plant has the endearing quality
of making babies on the edges of its leaves.
The non-pink original form was called
"mother of thousands", as its babies dropped
and sprouted everywhere. The pink ones
do not form roots as readily and so are not
a nuisance.

LIGHT PREFERENCE: This bright-pink
succulent needs plenty of light to keep its
bright pink coloring. A south or west window
is best.

WATERING: Plant this succulent in a
fast-draining potting mix, and let it dry
out a bit before watering again.

SIZE: It will grow to approximately 2 feet
(0.6 m) tall.

PROPAGATION: Take cuttings, allow them to
callus, and plant in a moist potting medium.

PINK QUILL

BOTANICAL NAME: *Tillandsia cyanea*

The pink bracts that produce the purple flowers are the main attraction of this bromeliad. When the flowers appear from the bract, they are small and do not last long. The pink bract, on the other hand, lasts for months. It will then turn brown and can be cut off. At this time, the parent plant will begin to fade but will be putting its last bit of energy into making offsets at its base. These can be grown to one-third to one-half the size of the parent, then cut off and potted individually, or they can be allowed to grow, eventually creating a large grouping of the plant. Quite often this plant is tossed like a poinsettia when its done blooming.

LIGHT PREFERENCE: A medium to bright light is best, especially if you are keeping the plant and would like the new plant to bloom.

WATERING: These plants are usually grown in a potting medium, unlike most epiphytic bromeliads. Water when the medium becomes dry.

FLOWER: The small purple flowers appear from the sides of the large pink bract.

SIZE: With the bract, the plant will not be more than 10 inches (25.4 cm) tall.

PROPAGATION: This can be grown from seed, or the offsets can be removed from the parent and potted up individually.

PLUM PINE, BUDDHIST PINE, SOUTHERN YEW

BOTANICAL NAME: *Podocarpus macrophyllus* var. *maki*

In much of the United States, this plant is grown outside and is used as an evergreen hedging plant, hence, the southern yew common name. In northern climes, it is used as a houseplant. The variety *maki* is most often used as a houseplant, as it stays more compact with shorter leaves. It can be kept smaller with pruning or made into a shaped topiary or even a bonsai.

LIGHT PREFERENCE: This plant prefers a medium to bright light but can tolerate low light, as well.

WATERING: Keep it evenly moist and plant in a fast-draining potting medium. Do not allow it to stand in water, as it is susceptible to root rot.

FLOWER: The pollen cones are white and catkin-like in shape and develop red berries. This most often will not happen in the home setting.

SIZE: The plant grows to 6 to 8 feet (1.8 to 2.4 m) but with pruning can be kept 4 to 5 feet (1.2 to 1.5 m) tall. It is an excellent large floor plant.

PROPAGATION: Take tip cuttings, dip in rooting hormone, and plant in a moist potting medium. They can also be grown from seed.

POLKA DOT PLANT

BOTANICAL NAME: *Hypoestes phyllostachya*

Polka dot plants are a smaller, endearing plant used quite often in dish gardens and terrariums. They are thin-leaved plants that need high humidity levels to grow their best. For this reason, make sure the humidity is high by using a pebble tray or placing in a terrarium.

LIGHT PREFERENCE: A medium light is best in an east window or back a few feet from a west window. If placed in an area where they get full-sun exposure, the thin leaves may become washed out or even burnt.

WATERING: Keep this plant evenly moist, not allowing it to dry out, as it quite unforgiving of dry soil. Place on a pebble tray or in a terrarium to keep the humidity high. Low humidity will cause brown leaf tips and edges.

FLOWER: The flowers are small and inconspicuous.

SIZE: These may reach 16 inches (40.6 cm) or more, but can become leggy, so trim to keep it full.

PROPAGATION: Tip cuttings rooted in moist potting mix, or it can be grown from seed.

PONYTAIL PALM, ELEPHANT FOOT

SIZE: This plant may reach 10 to 12 feet (3 to 3.7 m) in the house but only after many years. It prefers to be in a snug pot, and you will often find them in a pot just a little larger than the swollen caudex.

PROPAGATION: This plant may send up offshoots at the base of the plant, and these can be potted up individually.

BOTANICAL NAME: *Beaucarnea recurvata*

The swollen caudex (stem) is the trait of this plant that is usually noticed first. The appearance of the caudex is rough and cracked and because of the shape with these traits, may suggest an elephant's foot, thus the common name. The medium green-colored fountain of strappy leaves emerging from the top of the stem give it the ponytail name. The palm part is a mystery because in no way does this resemble a palm, nor is it related to them.

LIGHT PREFERENCE: Put this plant in as much light as you can. A south or west window is best.

WATERING: Plant in a fast-draining potting medium, as for cacti and other succulents. Allow the soil to dry out between waterings, and if you are in doubt, don't add water, as the swollen caudex holds water.

FLOWER: With enough sun, these plants do produce a large panicle of creamy white flowers but most likely this will not occur in the home environment.

POTHOS, DEVIL'S IVY

BOTANICAL NAME: *Epipremnum aureum*

This is the ultimate houseplant and its likely you, your parents, or your grandparents have had one. It has been seen framing windows, sprawling down furniture or spanning beams on the ceiling. It is an easy plant that can be kept under control with trimming. Its tolerance to low-light situations is definitely a plus in the houseplant world.

LIGHT PREFERENCE: The golden pothos that has green leaves with yellow marbling can tolerate low light such as a north window, but prefers a medium light within a few feet of a west or east window. If your plant reverts to an all-green plant, move it into more light and it will regain its variegation.

WATERING: This plant will let you know it is dry when every leaf wilts over the edge of the pot. Yet, it would be best if that never happens, as it will react by having some yellow leaves. Keep it evenly moist, but never standing in water as the roots may rot and the plant collapse, with no chance of revival.

FLOWER: This plant is grown for foliage and will not likely flower in our homes.

SIZE: In its native habitat, this vine can climb up a tree 40 to 70 feet (12.2 to 21.3 m). It may even be unrecognizable as its leaves become huge and deeply lobed. It is unlikely that will happen in our homes. The vines could become 10 to 20 feet (3 to 6.1 m) long if left untrimmed. The leaves may only be on the ends of the otherwise-naked stems. It is better to keep your plant trimmed and full. Cut a few of the stems back to the soil line, and new sprouts will appear.

PROPAGATION: Stem cuttings can be rooted easily in water or in potting medium.

CULTIVARS:

• **'MARBLE QUEEN'**—This cultivar has white-and-green-splotched leaves that are exceptionally attractive. This cultivar will need more light as it has a lot of white on the leaves, but not full sun as those white parts will burn.

• **'N' JOY' AND 'PEARLS AND JADE'**— These cultivars are similar with more organized white-and-green patches. 'Pearls and Jade' also has small dots of green that soften the edges of the different colors. Both are newer hybrids and are exceptional.

• **'NEON'**—A bright chartreuse green cultivar that brightens any room with its yellow-green color.

• **'SILVER SATIN'**—If you have a difficult spot, this is the plant for you! The thick leaves of gray-green with silver splotches are nearly indestructible and beautiful. They are drought tolerant because of the thick leaves and also tolerant of lower light levels.

PRIMULINA

An African violet cousin, primulina was previously known under the name *chirita*. The leaves of some primulinas are so decorative that if it never flowered, it wouldn't matter. However, the small trumpet-shaped flowers are an additional bonus to these charming plants.

LIGHT PREFERENCE: A medium light is preferred by primulinas, the same as their African violet cousins—because they prefer the same conditions, they could be equally happy on the same plant stand. An east window or near a west window is perfect.

WATERING: Plant in a well-drained, porous soil, keeping it evenly moist. These plants have thick succulent leaves, some more than others, and are forgiving of drying out briefly. Do not allow them to stand in water.

FLOWER: Small, up to 2-inch-long (5.1 cm), trumpet-shaped flowers appear on stems above the foliage in colors of yellow, white, lavender, and combinations of those colors.

SIZE: There are miniature varieties as well as plants that grow to several feet across. Most offered for sale stay about the size of an African violet.

PROPAGATION: Take a single leaf cutting and place in a moist potting medium, the same as you would for an African violet. It may benefit from being covered with plastic or glass. In a few weeks, small plants will appear at the base.

CULTIVARS:

• **'VIETNAMESE VIOLET'** *(PRIMULINA TAMIANA)*—A miniature plant perfect for a terrarium. It produces tiny white flowers with a purple throat.

PURPLE HEART

BOTANICAL NAME: *Setcreasea pallida*

This plant has become popular as an annual added to combination pots in the summer, but it has been a popular houseplant for some time as well. It has purple stems to match the purple leaves, and the stems are quite succulent. It has a drooping habit and is well suited as a hanging basket.

LIGHT PREFERENCE: This plant prefers a bright light and will thrive in a south or west window.

WATERING: Keep the soil evenly moist, though the plant is somewhat forgiving of drying out, because of its succulent stems.

FLOWER: Pink flowers appear in the depression where the two leaves cross. They are not large or conspicuous, but do add a touch of color to the all-purple plant.

SIZE: It can become 8 to 12 inches (20.3 to 30.5 cm) tall and spread up to 20 inches (50.8 cm).

PROPAGATION: Take tip cuttings and pot in a moist potting medium.

CULTIVARS: There is a variegated form with light purple stripes that is worth hunting down.

PURPLE PASSION PLANT, VELVET PLANT

BOTANICAL NAME: *Gynura aurantiaca*

The fuzzy hairs on this plant are its most endearing feature. The bright orange flowers are also endearing, but their smell is not. These vines can be cut back to keep them compact or allowed to wander and frame a window, if desired.

LIGHT PREFERENCE: To keep its purple coloring, this plant needs bright light. If it is green, move it into more light. An east or west window is best.

WATERING: Keep this plant evenly moist. If it is kept too wet, it will rot.

FLOWER: The flowers of the velvet plant are orange, but they have an unpleasant aroma so cutting them off while they are in bud is a good idea.

SIZE: This vining plant can become leggy. Keeping it trimmed back will make for a more attractive, bushy plant.

PROPAGATION: When you prune the vine back, use the cuttings to propagate new plants. Place them in a moist potting medium, and keep them reasonably moist until they root.

CULTIVARS:

- •**'VARIEGATA'**—A creamy white combined with purple and green on the leaves make this a gorgeous cultivar.

QUEEN'S TEARS, FRIENDSHIP PLANT

BOTANICAL NAME: *Billbergia nutans*

This epiphytic bromeliad is perfect for a bright window in the house. It produces flowers on long, drooping stems. This plant is most often sold growing in pots filled with coarse medium, such as that used for orchids. But they would be equally happy mounted on a piece of wood. Do not fertilize these plants, as it may cause the leaves to turn only green and lose their beautiful coloring. It produces plenty of offsets that are easily shared, giving it the name "friendship plant".

LIGHT PREFERENCE: Give it plenty of light in the house. It needs at least a medium light to bloom.

WATERING: Pour water into the vase of leaves, letting the overflow wet the medium. Empty it often and refill with fresh water to ensure there are no stains from water additives on the leaves. Stagnant water may also lead to disease.

SIZE: They range in size from 8 to 36 inches (20.3 to 91.4 cm) tall, depending on the species.

PROPAGATION: Billbergias send out offsets readily, and they can be separated and potted up or mounted individually.

RADIATOR PLANT

BOTANICAL NAME: *Peperomia maculosa*

The dark green, thick, leathery leaves make this an attractive plant. It prefers to be a bit pot-bound, so do not over-pot it.

LIGHT PREFERENCE: A medium light from an east or west window is preferred, but the low light of a north window works as well.

WATERING: Do not overwater this plant. Its thick succulent leaves hold water. If placed in low light, less water will be needed.

FLOWER: This plant is grown for its foliage.

SIZE: The radiator plant will stay under 10 inches (25.4 cm).

PROPAGATION: Propagate from cuttings.

ROCK FIG

BOTANICAL NAME: *Ficus petiolaris*

The enlarged stem or caudex of this ornamental fig adds to the interest of the plant. The leaves are medium green with pink veins. In its natural habitat, it grows over rocks, covering them with its roots—thus the name "rock fig." Any changes in its environment may cause it to drop leaves. It normally will regrow its leaves when accustomed to the new conditions. It is also used often as a bonsai plant.

LIGHT PREFERENCE: As with other members of the ficus/fig family, a high-light spot is needed. A south or west window is best.

WATERING: Keep this plant evenly moist.

FLOWER: Green flowers become small figs, but these will rarely appear in the home environment.

SIZE: In its native habitat, it may reach 20 to 30 feet (6.1 to 9.1 m) tall, but by keeping it trimmed, the plant can be less than 5 feet (1.5 m) tall in the house. It can also be kept smaller by reducing its container size, but this means you must then keep on top of the watering.

PROPAGATION: Tip cuttings can be taken and potted in a moist medium. It also can be grown from seed or air layered.

ROSARY VINE, CHAIN OF HEARTS, HEARTS ENTANGLED

BOTANICAL NAME: *Ceropegia woodii*

This succulent vine, covered with speckled, heart-shaped leaves, is adorable. When the tiny purple flowers appear, it makes it all the cuter. It is well suited to a hanging basket. The small tubers that appear along the stems can be used to propagate the plant and give rise to the common name of rosary vine.

LIGHT PREFERENCE: Give this plant as much sun as you can, otherwise the stems will elongate excessively between the leaves. Hang this plant in a south or west window.

WATERING: Water thoroughly and allow the potting medium to dry out a bit before watering again. Never allow it to stand in water.

FLOWER: The small, under 1-inch (2.5 cm) flowers, are pinkish tubes that face upward with a dark purple top. They appear from the leaf axils.

SIZE: The plant lies quite flat to the potting mix surface, but may hang as long as 10 feet (3 m) or more if there is room.

PROPAGATION: Small tubers grow along the stems and can be removed and placed on top of a moist potting medium, where they will form roots and send out stems. Tip cuttings can also be taken.

CULTIVARS:

• *CEROPEGIA WOODII* **'VARIEGATA'**— This cultivar adds some pink to its white-and-green leaves, and it is gorgeous!

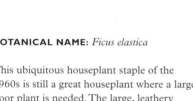

RUBBER PLANT

BOTANICAL NAME: *Ficus elastica*

This ubiquitous houseplant staple of the 1960s is still a great houseplant where a large floor plant is needed. The large, leathery leaves make a bold statement. It is known for its adaptability to low-light situations, but prefers a medium to bright light. If a leaf or stem is broken, a white, milky substance will appear. Stop the flow by placing a paper towel on the broken or cut end.

LIGHT PREFERENCE: A medium to bright light is best.

WATERING: Water thoroughly and allow the potting medium to become dry an inch or two down in the pot. Too much water will cause the lower leaves to yellow and fall off.

FLOWER: This plant will not likely flower in the house.

SIZE: In its natural habitat, this plant can grow to monstrous proportions up to 100 feet (30.5 m) tall. In the house, it may reach 10 feet (3 m) or more if given the room.

PROPAGATION: Tip cuttings can be taken, dried, and potted up in a moist potting medium. It will need bottom heat to grow roots. Air layering is also an effective way of making more plants and helps if your plant has become too tall.

CULTIVARS:

- **'BURGUNDY'**—A cultivar with dark burgundy, almost-black leaves.

- **'ROBUSTA'**—A dark green variety.

- **'RUBY'**—This variegated form has medium green leaves with pink edges.

- **'TINEKE'**—Another variegated variety but with white edges.

SAGO PALM

BOTANICAL NAME: *Cycas revoluta*

This plant does have a leaf that looks like a palm and has the word "palm" in its name, but it is not related to palms, rather to conifers. The leaves are made up of many leaflets with sharp points that should be avoided. The petiole or stems of the leaves have barbs on them. But even with the danger factor, this is a popular plant for its strong architectural presence. It is often offered as a bonsai. When it puts out new growth, it puts out a whole ring of leaves at the same time, and this usually happens every year. This is a very slow-growing plant. This plant is extremely toxic, so keep away from pets and children.

LIGHT PREFERENCE: Bright light with full sun, such as is available in a south window, is best. When the new leaves appear, they may be elongated from insufficient light.

WATERING: Water thoroughly and allow the medium to dry out partially before watering again.

FLOWER: Flowers do not usually appear on plants grown in the home.

SIZE: The plant can be 1 foot to 12 feet (0.3 to 3.7 m) in diameter in its natural habitat, but usually less than 2 to 3 feet (0.6 to 0.9 m) in the home.

PROPAGATION: Propagation is by seed or by removing the offsets from the base of the plant and potting them up individually.

SCARLET STAR

BOTANICAL NAME: *Guzmania lingulata*

This popular plant is easily found for sale, even in the grocery store. Its popularity is attributed to the beautiful colored bracts that last for many months. This bromeliad is found growing as an epiphyte on trees in the tropical rainforest, but is usually offered for sale in a container. Its leaves aren't spiny like others in the family, but soft. Used often in commercial settings, it is then discarded after the bracts fade.

LIGHT PREFERENCE: If bought with colorful bracts, this plant can be placed almost anywhere and enjoyed for months. If you would like for offsets to form and grow well, keep it in a medium to bright light.

WATERING: Fill the vase formed by the leaves with water, letting it overflow into the potting medium. Water only in the leaf vase, and don't let water sit in the flower head. Like other bromeliads, the parent plant will begin to die after flowering, sending up offsets at the base of the plant.

FLOWER: The flowers are small and inconspicuous compared to the colorful bracts that surround them.

SIZE: This plant can grow approximately 2 feet (0.6 m) tall.

PROPAGATION: The offsets that are formed by the parent plant after flowering can be separated and grown individually.

SCREW PINE

BOTANICAL NAME: *Pandanus veitchii*

The screw pine is a large plant with spines along the leaves. It grows very large and would need plenty of space in a home. The variety *Pandanus veitchii*, now available to the consumer, is a beautiful yellow variegated version with multiple crowns. These are free of spines and are offered at about 18 inches (45.7 cm) high. They make a very nice foil to plain-green plants. They are relatively slow growers, and do not have the usual spiraling form of the regular screw pines.

LIGHT PREFERENCE: In the home setting, the screw pine needs to be placed in high light such as in front of a south window.

WATERING: Keep the screw pine evenly moist. It naturally grows in moist areas.

FLOWER: It most likely will not bloom in your home but does produce flowers, which, in turn, produce fruits that resemble orange pinecones.

SIZE: These can become large trees in the wild, up to 20 feet (6.1 m) tall or more. The newer cultivars will probably not grow taller than a few feet, and they are choice plants for displaying on a pedestal or plinth.

PROPAGATION: Propagate by offsets at the base of the plant.

SHAVING BRUSH FLOWER

BOTANICAL NAME: *Haemanthus albiflos*

The bulb of this plant usually sits on top of the potting medium, adding to its interest. The leaves are rounded, and it produces two leaves at time. The flowers appear in late fall to winter and look like white shaving brushes with yellow tips. It is related to the more familiar amaryllis.

LIGHT PREFERENCE: Give the shaving brush flower a bright light but not full sun.

WATERING: Because of its water-storing bulb, the medium can be allowed to dry out quite a bit before watering again.

FLOWER: The flowers arise on short stalks and resemble an old-fashioned shaving brush. This bulb flowers better in snug quarters, so do not overpot.

SIZE: The plant grows 8 to 12 inches (20.3 to 30.5 cm) tall.

PROPAGATION: This plant produces offsets that can be carefully removed from the parent and potted individually.

SHOOTING STAR HOYA

BOTANICAL NAME: *Hoya multiflora*

Unlike many other hoyas, the shooting star is not a succulent. The leaves are thin and dark green. It does have pendulous stems and makes for a great hanging basket. The beautiful white-and-yellow flowers that resemble shooting stars may appear more than once in the year. This is an easy plant to grow and bloom.

LIGHT PREFERENCE: Bright light is needed to form flowers. A south or west window is best.

WATERING: Because this isn't a succulent, it will need more water than its other family members. Plant in a well-drained potting medium, and keep it evenly moist.

FLOWER: The clusters of white flowers resemble small shooting stars with yellow tails. As with most flowers of the hoya family, the nectar is excessive and drips off the tips of the flowers. With that in mind, place your plant where it won't drip on furniture or rugs.

SIZE: The stems may reach 4 to 5 feet (1.2 to 1.5 m), but they can be trimmed to keep the plant smaller.

PROPAGATION: Propagate from tip cuttings in moist potting medium.

SHOWY MEDINILLA, PINK LANTERN, ROSY GRAPE

BOTANICAL NAME: *Medinilla magnifica*

A well-grown blooming medinilla is a sight to behold. The pink flowers hanging down from the dark green foliage are show-stopping. In its native habitat, it most often grows as an epiphyte in trees. The leaves are large, heavily veined, and leathery.

LIGHT PREFERENCE: Place your medinilla in an east or west window. This plant needs bright light to produce flowers.

WATERING: Water thoroughly, and allow the plant to dry out partially before watering again. Raise the humidity by setting this plant on a pebble tray.

FLOWER: Hanging pink panicles of flowers descend out of large pink bracts.

SIZE: The plant grows up to 4 feet (1.2 m) tall.

PROPAGATION: If there are multiple plants in the pot, you can separate them and pot up individually. Or take tip cuttings with at least two leaves. Root in a moist potting medium. Cut off one-half of the large leaf to prevent water loss. Cover the pot with plastic or glass to keep the humidity up while it grows roots and leaves.

SHRIMP PLANT

PROPAGATION: Tip cuttings can be rooted in a moist potting medium.

CULTIVARS:

'YELLOW QUEEN'—Yellow bracts surround the white flowers.

'VARIEGATA'—This variety has the shrimp-colored flowers, and the foliage is variegated white and green.

BOTANICAL NAME: *Justicia brandegeana*

The bracts (or modified leaves) are slightly curved and shaped like shrimp; small white flowers peek out from between the bracts. The flowers are sometimes overlooked because the bracts are so showy. Even the color of the bracts reminds one of shrimp. This is an easy houseplant with unique characteristics.

LIGHT PREFERENCE: These plants need a medium to bright light to ensure blooms are formed.

WATERING: Keep the potting medium evenly moist. If the medium is kept too wet or too dry, it may drop its leaves.

FLOWER: The flowers are small white tubes that peek out of the colored bracts, which are a peachy-red color.

SIZE: In your home, the shrimp plant may be 1 to 3 feet (0.3 to 0.9 m) tall. It can get leggy, so keep it trimmed to keep it compact.

SILVER SPRINKLES

BOTANICAL NAME: *Pilea glauca*

This diminutive, low-growing plant is a nice groundcover. The small red stems hold up small silver leaves less than ¼ inch (0.6 cm) wide. It is a perfect terrarium or dish garden groundcover.

LIGHT PREFERENCE: This plant does need a medium light to stay compact and a bright light if it is growing in a terrarium.

WATERING: Keep it evenly moist. If left too dry, it will drop its leaves. It will do well in the humid environment of a terrarium if in enough light.

FLOWER: Tiny flower clusters rise a few inches above the foliage, but may not be seen in the home environment.

SIZE: This groundcover is 2 to 4 inches (5.1 to 10.2 cm) tall.

PROPAGATION: This spreading plant could be split apart and potted separately, or take tip cuttings and root in a moist medium.

SILVER SQUILL

BOTANICAL NAME: *Ledebouria socialis* (syn. *Scilla violacea*)

This small, bulbous plant has beautiful strappy leaves mottled with splotches of dark green. The underside of the leaf is a burgundy color. The bulb is usually sitting on top of the medium, adding to the uniqueness of this plant.

LIGHT PREFERENCE: Give the silver squill a bright light, such as a south or west window. If the light isn't bright enough, the leaves will stretch toward it.

WATERING: Water thoroughly and let the soil dry out partially before watering again. Because the bulbs above the medium store moisture, they can take a bit of dryness. Yet, if it is allowed to dry too much, the plant will lose leaves.

FLOWER: The tiny flowers are on stems that rise above the foliage an inch or two. Each flower is pink, green, and white, and quite beautiful; unfortunately, they are very small. When they bloom, find a magnifying glass, and look at them closely.

SIZE: This plant stays under 10 inches (25.4 cm) tall.

PROPAGATION: The plant multiplies rapidly and is easily pulled apart. They look better with a few pieces in one pot, instead of individually potted.

SILVER TREE

BOTANICAL NAME: *Pilea spruceana*

The bronze-and-silver leaves of this small houseplant are a welcome relief from an all-green palette. It is an easy-to-grow houseplant and is also suitable for a terrarium or miniature garden.

LIGHT PREFERENCE: A medium light is perfect for this plant, such as an east window.

WATERING: Water thoroughly and then again when the top 1 to 2 inches (2.5 to 5.1 cm) of the medium is dry. Err on the dry side for this plant, rather than keeping it too moist.

FLOWER: Flowers are inconspicuous.

SIZE: This is a smaller houseplant at 6 to 12 inches (15.2 to 30.5 cm).

PROFAGATION: Take tip cuttings and pot in a moist potting medium.

SLIPPER ORCHID

BOTANICAL NAME: *Paphiopedilum*

This orchid is easy to grow and good for beginner orchid growers. The flowers of the slipper orchid are so gorgeous and exotic looking, they may intimidate some from attempting to grow them. Fear not: they are quite easy and need care not unlike that of African violets. They may have marbled or mottled as well as solid-green leaves. Paphiopedilum having silver-mottled leaves are better suited to warm house temperatures than those having plain-green leaves that need cooler temperatures. The foliage makes it beautiful, even when the plant isn't flowering. Most are terrestrial, meaning they grow in organic matter as opposed to being epiphytic, or growing in trees.

LIGHT PREFERENCE: These orchids are considered low-light orchids in their native habitat, but will not bloom in a low-light area in our homes. A medium light, such as an east window, would be best for the flowering success of the plant, or grow it under electric lights.

WATERING: As with other orchids, watering practices depend on the medium the plant is growing in, temperature, and light levels. If growing in moss, wait until the moss has turned a lighter color at the surface. If growing in a finely chopped fir bark, then water when the color of the bark is not as dark as it was when first watered. They need to be watered regularly, as they have no means of storing water, unlike some orchids.

FLOWER: The flowers have a pouch on the front of the flower, giving it the look of a slipper and its common name. The flowers can last many weeks and come in many combinations of colors.

SIZE: The leaves are rarely higher than 6 inches (15.2 cm) and may be up to a 1 inch (2.5 cm) wide. The flowers rise up above the foliage 10 to 12 inches (25.4 to 30.5 cm).

PROPAGATION: The plant will make offsets, and these can be divided and potted up separately.

SNAKE PLANT, BOW STRING HEMP PLANT, MOTHER-IN-LAW'S TONGUE

BOTANICAL NAME: *Sansevieria trifasciata*

The snake plant family has certainly received a bad reputation as boring, ho-hum plants. Yet, grown well, they can be a beautiful plant with many forms and cultivars available. Previously placed in dark corners and allowed to languish, they have come into their own as air purifiers. This quality, along with better information about growing this plant, has given it the place in the houseplant world it deserves. It is tall, up to 4 feet (10.2 cm), and has green leaves with darker green markings.

LIGHT PREFERENCE: The snake plant will tolerate low-light situations but will thrive in a medium to bright light.

WATERING: Many a snake plant has been killed by overwatering. If they are in a low-light situation, water infrequently, letting the medium become quite dry before watering again. If in a high light, they will use more water. Never allow a sansevieria to stand in water. Rotten snake plants are slimy and smell horrible.

FLOWER: If given enough light, a stem will appear from the plant and aromatic white flowers will follow.

SIZE: These plants can be a few inches tall to many feet tall. There are many cultivars available.

PROPAGATION: Because of the multiple crowns this plant produces, separating is the simplest way to propagate them. Leaves cut into 2 to 3 inch (5.1 to 7.6 cm) sections and planted upright will form new plants at the base. Make sure the sections are planted with the top side up or they will not grow.

CULTIVARS:

- **'FERNWOOD'** —This is a newer variety, resembling a small cylindrica form, but its leaves are not completely round. Its mottled foliage is attractive. It grows to around 2 feet (0.6 m).

- **S. CYLINDRICA**—Instead of flat leaves, this plant's leaves are round and very sharply pointed. It can grow to over 6 feet (1.8 m).

- **'BANTEL'S SENSATION'**—The bright white-and-green-striped leaves of this cultivar are very striking. It will be 3 to 4 feet (0.9 to 1.2 m) tall.

- **'TWISTER'**—Its undulating, twisting leaves make this an interesting specimen. It will grow up to 12 inches (30.5 cm) tall.

- **'GOLD FLAME'**—It has bright-yellow leaves with dark-green stripes.

- **'LAURENTII'**—This green-striped variety with yellow edges is a very popular old cultivar, growing 3 to 4 feet (0.9 to 1.2 m) tall.

- **'MASON'S CONGO' (S. MASONIANA)**—The leaves of this large variety can be 8 to 10 inches (20.3 to 25.4 cm) wide and the plant can grow 3 to 4 feet (0.9 to 1.2 m) tall.

FLOWER: The flowers are little green bells that hang down from the underside of the stems. They are almost impossible to detect but are fascinating if you notice them.

SIZE: This plant may get 1 to 3 feet (0.3 to 0.9 m) tall and wide.

PROPAGATION: Take tip cuttings and root in a moist potting medium with bottom heat and cover to keep humidity high.

SNOW BUSH

BOTANICAL NAME: *Breynia disticha roseo-picta*

The highly variegated leaves of this plant are mottled with white-and-pink splotches; the pink color is most concentrated in the tips of the branches, making it seem as if they have flowers. The white variegation gives the effect that snow has fallen on the plant, hence the common name. The stems are a reddish color and wiry. It needs to be kept well-watered or the small leaves will fall off. Keep the tips pinched to keep the plant compact.

LIGHT PREFERENCE: Give this plant a bright light to keep the color at its best and to promote flowering.

WATERING: Keep it evenly moist, never letting it completely dry out, or the leaves will fall off. Keep the humidity up by placing the plant on a pebble tray.

SPIDER PLANT, AIRPLANE PLANT

BOTANICAL NAME: *Chlorophytum comosum*

The much-loved spider plant is one of the most popular houseplants grown. The variegated version is usually the one offered for sale and most often in a hanging basket. The miniature plants floating in the air attached to long stems from the parent are the most endearing characteristic of this plant. The tuberous root system means it will need to be up-potted or divided when the roots fill the pot or it may break the container.

LIGHT PREFERENCE: The solid-green version of this plant could take low light, but the variegated versions need a medium to bright light.

WATERING: Keep the spider plant evenly moist. Brown tips appear due to salt buildup from fertilizing the plant. Flush the plant often to rectify the problem, and trim the leaves to remove the brown tips.

FLOWER: Small, star-shaped, white flowers appear in conjunction with the small plants at the end of the stems. They are not extremely showy, but are delicate and pretty.

SIZE: The plants are 1 to 2 feet (0.3 to 0.6 m) tall, but the stems cascade 2 to 3 feet (0.6 to 0.9 m) over the edge of the container.

PROPAGATION: The little plantlets at the ends of the stems can be removed and rooted in a moist potting medium. To ensure faster rooting, leave the babies attached to the parent plant and pin them to a container of moist medium. When they are well rooted, cut them away from the parent. You can also divide a large plant into smaller pieces and pot each individually.

CULTIVAR:

• **'BONNIE'**—This cultivar has curly leaves.

STICKS ON FIRE, PENCIL CACTUS

BOTANICAL NAME: *Euphorbia tirucalli*

The all-green version of this succulent plant is called "pencil cactus" as its stems are approximately the size and shape of pencils. The cactus part is a mystery as it is a succulent member of the spurge family with no spines at all. The newer variety has been hybridized to have red ends and so has the name "sticks on fire." It has become popular to use this plant as the "thriller" in the center of full-sun combination pots. Without the bright light or full sun it would receive outside, the red tips may not "burn" in our homes, but it is a unique plant to grow on a bright windowsill. Be careful when handling, as its white sap is irritating.

LIGHT PREFERENCE: Give these succulents as much light as possible, especially with the red variety or otherwise it will turn green.

WATERING: Plant in a fast-draining potting medium, allowing it to become quite dry between waterings.

FLOWER: This plant will most likely not flower in the house.

SIZE: In its natural habitat, it could grow to a 30-foot-tall (9.1 m) shrub, but in your home may reach the ceiling. It can be trimmed to keep it smaller.

PROPAGATION: Remove a segment of the plant, allow it to callus over, then place it in a moist medium to root.

STRIPED INCH PLANT

BOTANICAL NAME: *Callisia elegans*

This is a creeping plant than can quickly cover a large area, making it perfect for a hanging basket. The medium-green leaves are covered with delicate white lines. It can become lanky, so keep it trimmed and use the cuttings for new plants.

LIGHT PREFERENCE: A medium to bright light is best.

WATERING: Keep it evenly moist.

FLOWER: Tiny white flowers appear with enough light.

SIZE: This vine rarely grows higher than 6 inches (15.2 cm) but spreads much further.

PROPAGATION: It is easily propagated by stem cuttings placed in moist potting medium.

SWISS CHEESE PLANT, FRUIT SALAD PLANT

BOTANICAL NAME: *Monstera deliciosa*

This large plant, like the rubber plant, was a staple of the mid-century decorating scheme. The high ceilings and open-concept floor plan that is popular today has brought this large plant back with a vengeance. It is now one of the most popular plants for its large architectural presence and ease of care. The large, perforated, lobed leaves are unique: They are thought to have holes in the leaves to combat the strong winds and large amounts of rain they can be exposed to high in the trees of the rainforest. They do send out aerial roots to gather more moisture and to stabilize themselves. Do not allow them to attach themselves to your wood floors or other surfaces, as they will leave marks when pulled away.

LIGHT PREFERENCE: Monstera can tolerate low light, but prefers a medium to bright light. In their native habitat, they start life on the jungle floor and scramble along until they find a tree to cling to, then climb to the top for light.

WATERING: Keep this plant evenly moist, letting it get quite dry before watering again.

FLOWER: The flower most likely will not appear in the house. It gets its name "fruit salad" because the ripe fruit—which resembles an ear of corn—is edible and said to taste like a cross between banana and pineapple. The unripe fruit is not edible and may cause irritation to the mouth and throat.

SIZE: This plant can get quite large and will need a lot of room to grow. Growing it on a moss pole is best so it has something to cling to. It may reach 10 feet (3 m) or taller.

PROPAGATION: Propagate by stem tip cuttings potted in moist potting medium. It can also be air layered.

CULTIVAR:

• **'VARIEGATA'**—A variegated form that has splotches of light-green and white on the dark-green leaves.

SWISS CHEESE VINE

BOTANICAL NAME: *Monstera friedrichsthalii* (syn. *Monstera adansonii*)

This plant shares its name with the Swiss cheese plant but is a much smaller vine and has leaves with solid edges, and the leaf itself is filled with perforations. It's a good alternative to the extremely large *deliciosa* and yet has similar unique leaves.

LIGHT PREFERENCE: This plant will take a low light, but prefers a medium to bright light.

WATERING: Water thoroughly and let it dry a bit, but not completely, before watering again.

FLOWER: It most likely will not flower in the home.

SIZE: This vining plant likes a moss pole to climb and will reach up to 6 feet (1.8 m).

PROPAGATION: Stem cuttings can be potted in a moist potting medium.

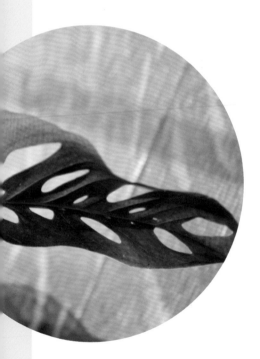

TEDDY BEAR PLANT, PANDA PLANT

BOTANICAL NAME: *Kalanchoe tomentosa*

This fuzzy succulent is loved by children and adults alike. Children like to pet the leaves, which are mostly covered with silver fuzz with brown accents on their edges.

LIGHT PREFERENCE: Give this succulent as much sun as possible. A south or west windowsill would be best.

WATERING: This succulent needs a well-drained potting medium. Let it dry down a bit before watering again.

FLOWER: It is unlikely the yellow-green flowers will appear in the home setting.

SIZE: It can grow 1 to 3 feet (0.3 to 0.9 m) tall.

PROPAGATION: Leaf cuttings should be allowed to callus over before planting in a moist potting soil.

CULTIVAR:

'CHOCOLATE SOLDIER'—Instead of having small rust-colored markings on the edges of the leaves, the whole leaf is rust colored.

TRAILING WATERMELON BEGONIA, RAINBOW VINE

BOTANICAL NAME: *Pellionia repens*

The dark burgundy edges and marbled middle give the appearance of a watermelon rind, giving this plant its common name. It's a low-growing vine that is perfect for a terrarium if the light is bright enough.

LIGHT PREFERENCE: To keep the rich burgundy color of the leaves, give this plant a medium to bright light. An east or west window is perfect.

WATERING: Keep this plant evenly moist to prevent leaf drop.

FLOWER: Small white clusters of flowers rise above the foliage a couple of inches. They are not showy.

SIZE: This mat-forming plant rarely exceeds 2 to 3 inches (5.1 to 7.6 cm) tall, but can trail up to a foot (0.3 m).

PROPAGATION: Tip cuttings are easily rooted in a moist potting medium.

TREE PHILODENDRON

BOTANICAL NAME: *Philodendron selloum* (syn. *Philodendron bipinnatifidum*)

This is another architectural plant popular for a large room setting. The leaves can be up to 4 feet (1.2 m) long. It's an easy plant to grow as long as it isn't overwatered.

LIGHT PREFERENCE: These large plants can tolerate a low-light situation but prefer a medium light, such as in an east or west window.

WATERING: Keep the potting medium evenly moist.

FLOWER: The white flowers probably will not appear in the home setting.

SIZE: This plant could reach proportions of up to 10 feet (3 m) wide and tall, but may not achieve that size in the house.

PROPAGATION: Propagate by taking tip cuttings and rooting in a moist potting medium.

UMBRELLA TREE

BOTANICAL NAME: *Schefflera actinophylla*

The umbrella tree is a large plant with palmate leaves that can reach a foot (0.3 m) or more across. If you have a large room with bright light, this is the plant for you. It is quite easy to grow and makes quite a statement.

LIGHT PREFERENCE: Keep your plant in a medium to bright spot, especially if it's the variegated version, to keep the color bright. If it starts to get leggy, move it into a brighter light.

WATERING: Keep this plant evenly moist, never letting it dry out. Occasionally take it to the shower if possible and spray it down to keep it clean. Otherwise, it is difficult to wash each individual leaf. Do not let it stand in water as the results will be yellow, dropping leaves.

FLOWER: The bright red spikes of flowers will not appear in the home setting.

SIZE: In its natural habitat, these trees can reach up to 40 feet (12.2 m) tall. In your home, it can be kept under 10 feet (3 m) with pruning.

PROPAGATION: Take cuttings of the stem tips and pot in a moist potting medium.

CULTIVARS:

- **'AMATE'**—This cultivar has been bred for better disease and insect resistance for the interior plant industry. It also does better in low-light conditions.

- **'AMATE SOLEIL'**—This variety has a vivid chartreuse color and brightens up any interior.

VARIEGATED SABER FIG, BANANA LEAF FIG

FLOWER: It is unlikely to bloom in the home.

SIZE: This plant could grow up to 10 feet (3 m) or more.

PROPAGATION: It can be propagated from cuttings, but may take a couple of months. Air layering can also be used.

BOTANICAL NAME: *Ficus maclellandii* 'Alii Variegated'

The strappy leaf version of the weeping fig is much easier to grow than the regular weeping fig. It does not drop leaves when it is stressed, such as being moved across the room. The bright chartreuse color of the leaves with dark- green splotches in their middles adds a bright spot to any room. The plain-green version would be easier to locate for purchase and is usually found as a tree-form standard. It also can take a lower light level, as it has no variegation.

LIGHT PREFERENCE: This plant needs a medium to bright light. The bright light will keep the color of the plant vibrant.

WATERING: Keep this plant evenly moist, not standing in water. If the plant dries out, some leaves may drop.

VARIEGATED STROMANTHE

BOTANICAL NAME: *Stromanthe sanguinea* 'Triostar'

The variegated green-and-white leaves with burgundy undersides of this plant are stunning. At night, they fold up like a prayer plant, a relative in the Marantaceae family. This plant is quite often used outside in the summer in mixed combination pots for shady situations. The white parts of the leaves will burn in full sun. In the house, though, it will need a bright light to keep its colors.

LIGHT PREFERENCE: Keep this plant in bright light to keep the colors of its foliage bright. A western exposure would be best.

WATERING: Keep this plant evenly moist, never dry, but not standing in water. They definitely need high humidity, so stand the pot on a pebble tray.

FLOWER: The reddish flowers are held above the foliage, but most likely won't occur in the home.

SIZE: It can reach 2 to 3 feet (0.6 to 0.9 m) tall and 1 to 2 feet (0.3 to 0.6 m) wide.

PROPAGATION: This plant naturally forms clumps, so divide the plant and pot up divisions individually.

FLOWER: The pink flowers are clustered in a half-ball shapes, like an upside-down umbrella. The flowers are baby pink with burgundy centers. When they flower, do not trim off the spur the flower came from, as it will flower in the same place again.

SIZE: This vine can get quite long and, if not in a hanging container, it could be trained on a trellis or as a wreath shape.

PROPAGATION: Take stem cuttings and root in a moist potting medium.

VARIEGATED WAX VINE, WAX FLOWER

BOTANICAL NAME: *Hoya carnosa* 'Tricolor'

The hoya flowers, when they appear, are gorgeous and look unreal, thus the wax flower name. The green leaves have white-and-pink edges. They are easily found to purchase and easy to grow.

LIGHT PREFERENCE: If you would like to see the gorgeous pink flowers, this succulent vine will need a bright light such as a south or west window. This plant does not like to be cold, so keep it in a warm spot.

WATERING: This is a succulent vine and so likes to be watered thoroughly and allowed to dry a bit before watering again. If the leaves begin to wrinkle, it has become too dry. In the lower light levels in the winter, wait longer between waterings. Do not allow it to stand in water.

VELDT GRAPE

BOTANICAL NAME: *Cissus quadrangularis*

This unusual plant has four-sided stems, which grow as long as they are allowed. It is often grown in a hanging basket. Its succulent stems grow in segments that can be easily separated and propagated. It is a plant that looks like no other: in the grape family, it grows leaves that resemble tiny grape leaves where the segments meet.

LIGHT PREFERENCE: Give this plant a bright light.

WATERING: This succulent can be allowed to become quite dry between waterings. If it is kept well-watered, it will have tiny grape-like leaves.

FLOWER: It does flower but most likely not in the home.

SIZE: These many-stemmed plants can grow as long as allowed.

PROPAGATION: Separate the segments, let them callus over, and plant them in a moist potting medium.

FLOWER: The lavender flowers are tiny and three-petaled, but they rarely bloom indoors.

SIZE: This vine typically doesn't grow taller than 6 inches (15 cm), but can trail 2 feet (0.6 m) long and more.

WANDERING JEW

PROPAGATION: Take stem cuttings and root in a moist potting medium.

BOTANICAL NAME: *Tradescantia zebrina*

This vine is a popular hanging basket plant. The attractive, iridescent, striped leaves shimmer in the light. It's an easy-to-grow plant and is often used outside in the summer. It is not easily moved inside from outside, however, so take cuttings and start over instead for best results.

LIGHT PREFERENCE: This plant does best in a medium to bright light. An east or west window works well.

WATERING: Keep the potting medium evenly moist, but not too wet. If it is too wet, stem and root rot can set in. Because the stems are succulent, it is forgiving of drying out temporarily.

WATERMELON PEPEROMIA

BOTANICAL NAME: *Peperomia argyreia*

Once you've seen this plant, the common name will make perfect sense. It looks just like the rind of a watermelon. The silver leaves have green stripes and a teardrop shape with red stems. These small, colorful plants are easy to grow as long as they don't become waterlogged.

LIGHT PREFERENCE: Give them a medium to bright light such as an east or west window.

WATERING: Keep the potting medium evenly moist but not wet, as the plants easily rot. Let the medium dry down a bit before watering again.

FLOWER: The slim stalks rise above the foliage and look like little greenish mouse tails. They are inconspicuous.

SIZE: It will grow 6 to 12 inches (15.2 to 30.5 cm) tall.

PROPAGATION: This plant can be propagated from a leaf cutting like an African violet. Place in a moist potting medium and cover with plastic or glass but watch the humidity levels so that the leaf doesn't rot. Small plants will appear at the base of the leaf.

WATERMELON VINE

SIZE: The plant is only a couple of inches high and spreads or hangs down from the container about 1 foot (0.3 m). If it gets leggy, pinch the ends off and use them to make more.

PROPAGATION: Take tip cuttings and root them in a moist potting medium.

BOTANICAL NAME: *Pellionia pulchra*

The watermelon vine has veining on its leaves that resembles a watermelon rind, and, to top it off, it has reddish stems. It is quite often used in terrariums and vivariums. It is usually sold as either a small plant for a terrarium or as a large plant in a hanging basket. This is an easy vine to grow. Though called a vine, it is more of a trailing plant.

LIGHT PREFERENCE: This vine needs only a low to medium light to be happy.

WATERING: It appreciates an evenly moist potting medium. If it becomes too dry, it will lose its older leaves. It does not want to stand in water, either.

FLOWER: Small clusters of tiny cream flowers rise on stems about 2 inches (5.1 cm) above the foliage. They are not showy and may not be noticed.

WEEPING FIG

BOTANICAL NAME: *Ficus benjamina*

This popular plant graces many mall plantings and can become stately in large inside spaces. These trees can become large in their natural habitat, up to 50 feet (15.2 m) tall and could become a tall tree in your home, but trimming it will keep it a reasonable size. They are known for dropping leaves but only do this when their environment changes. Once it acclimates to the changes, it will settle in and grow nicely. This tree has small leaves, so even though it is a large tree, it provides a softer look instead of an architectural statement. Find one with a braided stem for added interest.

LIGHT PREFERENCE: Although this plant can live in low-light situations, it will be fuller and grow better in a bright light, even full sun.

WATERING: Keep this plant evenly watered. Remember, changes in growing situations will cause it to drop leaves. Drying out and overwatering will trigger this, so try to keep it evenly moist.

FLOWER: It rarely flowers indoors.

SIZE: This plant is normally in the 2 to 10 feet (0.6 to 3 m) range indoors.

PROPAGATION: Tip cuttings may root in a moist medium, or the plant can be air layered.

CULTIVARS:

• **'NEON MARGUERITE'**—A variety with darker green blotches on bright chartreuse leaves. The older leaves turn to a darker green.

• **'STARLIGHT'**—A beautiful green variety with lots of white variegation.

FLOWER: White flowers are produced in the wild, but most likely not in the home.

SIZE: Although this plant can become large in its natural habitat, in the home situation, 6 to 7 feet (1.8 to 2.1 m) is the height to expect.

PROPAGATION: Cut a shoot off the cane, let it callus over, and then plant in a moist potting medium. The canes can be cut into pieces, allowed to dry, and planted in a moist potting medium.

YUCCA CANE

BOTANICAL NAME: *Yucca guatemalensis* (syn. *Yucca elephantipes*)

The plants have a coarse texture and are usually offered for sale in containers with three sizes of canes, to make for a fuller, more attractive plant. The bold look adds to a modern home setting and is gaining in popularity. Its relative ease of care adds to its popularity.

LIGHT PREFERENCE: Give this plant as much sun as you can. A south-facing window with plenty of sun would be best for this plant. It may do okay in lower light levels, but quite often the leaves will flop, losing their upright look.

WATERING: Water thoroughly, and allow the potting medium to dry down quite a bit before watering again. Plant in a fast-draining potting medium. Never leave it standing in water or keep it overly wet.

ZEBRA BASKET VINE

BOTANICAL NAME: *Aeschynanthus marmoratus*

The foliage of this attractive vine is medium green and has dark-green marbling throughout, with beige undersides covered with burgundy markings. It is a cousin of the African violet, also in the Gesneriad family. Give it a warm spot with plenty of bright light, and you may even be rewarded with the interesting greenish-yellow, tubular flowers. The plant is usually offered for sale in a hanging basket.

LIGHT PREFERENCE: Give this vine a medium light, such as is found in an east or west window.

WATERING: Keep the potting medium evenly moist.

FLOWER: The flower is tubular, upward-facing, and a greenish-yellow color. They are hard to see in the foliage, as they don't offer much color contrast, but are attractive.

SIZE: The vine is quite flat to the pot, usually only a couple of inches high, but the stems trail over the rim of the pot 1 to 2 feet (0.3 to 0.6 m).

PROPAGATION: Take tip cuttings and root them in moist potting medium.

ZEBRA PLANT

BOTANICAL NAME: *Haworthia fasciata*

The white tubercles (small, rounded protuberances) that cover the leaves of this small plant occur in a stripe-like pattern— hence the zebra name. Haworthia plants as a group are great houseplants, as they can take lower light levels than other succulents, and they have interesting patterns on their foliage.

LIGHT PREFERENCE: Place these small succulents on an east or west windowsill for the best results.

WATERING: Water thoroughly, and then allow the medium to dry a bit before watering again. Do not let these plants stand in water, and they will need less water in the winter when the light levels are low.

FLOWER: Long stems arise from the middle of the plant and small white flowers dangle from them. They aren't showy but are an added bonus.

SIZE: This small succulent can be from 2 to 8 inches (5.1 to 20.3 cm) tall.

PROPAGATION: These plants produce offsets that can be separated and planted individually.

ZZ PLANT

BOTANICAL NAME: *Zamioculcas zamiifolia*

This has become one of the most popular houseplants in the past few years, as it can take low light and still look amazing. This plant has shiny, dark-green leaves with a strong architectural appearance. The leaves are upright and are made up of many leaflets on each rachis (stem of a compound leaf), the actual "stem" being the underground tuberous rhizomes. The unusual part of this plant is that it can grow new plants from an individual leaflet, but it takes quite a long time.

LIGHT PREFERENCE: While it is true this plant can tolerate low light levels for quite some time, it prefers a medium to bright light to grow well.

WATERING: This plant has been touted as extremely drought tolerant, and whereas it can take long periods between waterings, this depends on the level of light it is growing in. If it dries down too much, it will drop leaflets.

FLOWER: The flower may appear, consisting of a white spadix surrounded by a white spathe. This may not happen in the home, but as this plant is grown for its beautiful foliage, the flowers would be an added bonus.

SIZE: This plant can reach up to 3 feet (0.9 m) tall.

PROPAGATION: As mentioned before, this plant can be propagated from one leaflet. Place the cut end into moist potting medium and cover with plastic or glass. This process may take many months. The plant can also be divided.

AFRICAN VIOLET

BOTANICAL NAME: *Saintpaulia*

African violets have received a bad rap as a grandma plant. Maybe your grandma did raise them, but they have come a long way since then. The number of colors, sizes, and leaf variations is mind-boggling. They have been hybridized to have yellow flowers, chimera flowers, and leaves, and so much more. Give this "grandma plant" another look.

LIGHT PREFERENCE: An east or west window is the best for African violets. Growing them under electric lights for 12 hours a day helps with symmetry and flowering.

WATERING: Keep your African violet evenly moist. Wick watering is a popular way to keep violets moist at all times. If your violet dries out and the growing medium pulls away from the sides of the pot, immerse it in water to rehydrate the medium.

FLOWER: Flowers range from yellow to purple with red, pink, green, and white in between. There are single, double, and semi-double flower types.

SIZE: There are standard, semi-miniature, and miniature plants. These range in size from 3 inches (7.6 cm) to 16 inches (40.6 cm) in diameter. Since the African Violet Society of America formed in 1946, the hybridizing of African violets has created more hybrids than can be kept track of.

PROPAGATION: The easiest way to propagate African violets is to simply cut a leaf off and pot it up in a potting media. Leave a 1-inch (2.5 cm) stem on the leaf and insert it at a 45-degree angle into the medium, making sure to keep the medium moist. In 6 to 8 weeks, baby plants should be ready to be removed and planted separately in their own pots.

ARTILLERY PLANT

BOTANICAL NAME: *Pilea microphylla*

The fine texture of this plant gives it a ferny appearance. The name comes from the way the plant ejects pollen from its small flowers. The diminutive size of the leaves and the plant make it a perfect fairy garden addition. Pinch it back to keep it bushy and smaller.

LIGHT PREFERENCE: A medium light is best, such as in an east or west window.

WATERING: Keep evenly moist, watering when the top of the potting medium feels dry. Do not keep it overly wet, as it easily rots.

FLOWER: Tiny greenish flowers are inconspicuous.

SIZE: This grows 8 to 12 inches (20.3 to 30.5 cm) tall.

PROPAGATION: Propagate from stem cuttings potted in moist medium.

CULTIVAR:

• **'VARIEGATA'**—A cultivar with green, white, and pink leaves.

BABY'S TEARS, MIND-YOUR-OWN-BUSINESS

BOTANICAL NAME: *Soleirolia soleirolii*

This is a creeping plant that will cover the container it is growing in and spill over the rim. It needs a potting medium to live on, so won't go too far down the container. This plant loves moisture and humidity so it makes a great terrarium plant. It can be used to cover a stuffed topiary frame as long as it is kept well-watered.

LIGHT PREFERENCE: It will grow in low light but prefers a medium light. An east or west window would be perfect.

WATERING: This plant prefers to be on the moist side at all times. Do not let it dry out. Raise the humidity as well by placing it on a pebble tray.

FLOWER: It may produce tiny white flowers if it has enough light.

SIZE: This plant grows close to the medium level so it can be a few inches high, but it spreads only as far as the container will allow it to.

PROPAGATION: Divide the plant into smaller clumps and pot individually.

BEEFSTEAK
BEGONIA

BOTANICAL NAME: *Begonia erythrophylla*

The beefsteak begonia is a plant your grandparents may have had. It is an older variety, but beautiful. This is an example of a rhizomatous begonia and it, like others in that group, have thick, succulent stems that grow over the soil surface, sending out foliage on the top of the stem and roots on the bottom. This particular begonia has large round leaves that are dark green with a burgundy underside; they resemble large lily pads. In the winter, they will send up a spray of delicate flowers.

LIGHT PREFERENCE: This begonia can grow in a north window but may not bloom and prefers an eastern exposure.

WATERING: Water the begonia thoroughly, never allowing it to stand in water. Then let it dry out a bit before watering again. Err on the dry side with this plant to avoid rotting. Use a well-drained potting medium.

FLOWER: In the wintertime, sprays of delicate flowers are on stems above the plant. They can be a light pink to white.

SIZE: This can become quite a sizeable begonia, at least 2 feet (0.6 m) tall and 2 to 3 feet (0.6 to 0.9 m) wide.

PROPAGATION: Take cuttings of the succulent stem and pin the sections to a moist medium.

CULTIVAR: Not a cultivar of the beefsteak, but another rhizomatous begonia is 'Madame Queen.' It displays the same dark-green leaf with burgundy undersides, but has an extremely ruffled edge that displays the burgundy underside on the top edge of the leaf.

SIZE: These ferns get quite large in their native habitats and can grow 4 feet (1.2 m) high and 3 feet (0.9 m) wide in your home if the conditions are favorable.

PROPAGATION: Spores that appear on the back of the fronds can be sown.

CULTIVARS:

- **'VICTORIA'**—A cultivar that has thinner leaves with wavy edges like a fluted piecrust.

- **'CRISPY WAVE'**—This cultivar has leaves that are entirely wavy, not just along the edges like the 'Victoria.'

BIRD'S NEST
FERN

BOTANICAL NAME: *Asplenium nidus*

This bright green fern probably does not resemble the picture you have in your mind of a typical fern. The fronds are an entire leaf, with no leaflets on the frond. Instead, the fronds of this fern form a bowl shape that has a "nest" made from a brown fuzzy substance from which arise the new fronds. As the fronds form, the round shape of the unfurling fronds look like small "eggs" in the "nest." It's a beautiful fern with an unusual shape.

LIGHT PREFERENCE: Place this fern in a medium light. An east window would be best, but they will grow in a north window as well.

WATERING: Keep this fern evenly moist, never allowing it dry out completely. Keep it out of standing water and raise the humidity by setting it on a pebble tray. Water around the edge of the pot, never in the center of the "nest" as it may rot the plant.

FLOWER: Ferns do not produce flowers.

BLEEDING HEART VINE

BOTANICAL NAME: *Clerodendrum thomsoniae*

This vine sends out white calyxes with red corollas protruding from their middles, giving it the name of "bleeding heart." This plant likes a winter rest with cooler temperatures. It may lose a lot of its leaves at this time, but they will regrow when it warms up. Water just enough to keep it from completely drying out until new growth begins.

LIGHT PREFERENCE: Give this vine plenty of sun to allow for flower formation.

WATERING: Keep this plant evenly moist. In good light and warmth, this vine will need plenty of water. Do not let it stand in water or completely dry out.

FLOWER: The plant will produce white, three-dimensional calyxes shaped like hearts with red corollas protruding out of the middle.

SIZE: This vine can grow 12 to 15 feet (3.7 to 4.6 m) long but can be kept smaller with pruning. Don't be afraid to prune, as the plant blooms on new growth. It can also be trained as a wreath.

PROPAGATION: Stem cuttings can be taken and potted in a moist potting medium covered with plastic to keep the humidity high while they are rooting.

BOSTON FERN

BOTANICAL NAME: *Nephrolepis exaltata* 'Bostoniensis'

This popular fern is an easy houseplant, as long as you can provide it with good light and plenty of humidity. Many admire this fern, grow it outside all summer, and yet, when they bring it in the house, are disappointed when it drops leaflets like crazy. This is normal, especially as it acclimates from the light levels and humidity outside to the lower levels in our dry, dark homes. Acclimating the fern to lower light levels before bringing it inside will help reduce the number of leaflets dropped. Yet, even one that has always been a houseplant is going to drop some leaflets in its normal aging process. This is a beautiful airy plant and worth a little clean up. Place it on a pedestal to show off its airy, arching fronds.

LIGHT PREFERENCE: Ferns in general love a medium light. They can tolerate low light such as a north window provides, though the medium light in an east window would be its preference.

WATERING: Keep this fern evenly moist, never allowing it to dry out. Use a potting medium with plenty of peat, yet with good drainage. Place on a pebble tray to raise the humidity.

FLOWER: Ferns do not produce flowers.

SIZE: This is a large fern that can become 3 feet (0.9 m) tall and wide.

PROPAGATION: This fern can be divided and potted up individually. It may also be propagated from the long runners it sends out. Pin them to a container of moist potting medium while still attached to the parent. With time, a new plant will form.

CULTIVARS:

• **COTTON CANDY FERN (*NEPHROLEPIS EXALTATA* 'SUZY WONG')** —A fluffy, foamy fern that does resemble swirls of cotton candy. This is a newer variety that also needs plenty of water and humidity.

• **LEMON BUTTON FERN (*N. EXALTATA* 'LEMON BUTTON')** —The leaflets of this diminutive fern are round like buttons and are staggered up the frond, overlapping each other. This cultivar also needs moisture and humidity.

• **RITA'S GOLD FERN (*N. EXALTATA* 'RITA'S GOLD')** —This bright chartreuse fern was discovered by Rita Randolph and, after giving a piece to Alan Armitage, it was trialed and he named it 'Rita's Gold.' An exceptional variety that adds a bright spot to any room. It is also used extensively in shady combination containers outside.

• **'TIGER FERN' (*N. EXALTATA*)** —A cultivar with striking variegation on the fronds.

BRAKE FERN, SILVER RIBBON FERN, TABLE FERN

BOTANICAL NAME: *Pteris cretica* 'Albolineata'

This is a unique fern that has fronds with one to five pairs of pinnae (the primary division of a fern frond) that look more like ribbons than the leaflets normally seen on ferns. This cultivar has a white stripe running down the center of the light green fronds. It mixes well with other ferns as it has such a different look.

LIGHT PREFERENCE: A medium to bright light is best, such as an east window or set back a bit from a west window. It really does not like a north window and may lose some of its variegation in the lower light.

WATERING: As with most ferns, keep it evenly moist, never allowing it to dry out or stand in water. Raise the humidity by placing it on a pebble tray.

FLOWER: Ferns do not flower.

SIZE: This is a smaller fern and grows 1 to 2 feet (0.3 to 0.6 m) tall and wide.

PROPAGATION: The plant may be divided to propagate.

RELATED FERN:

• **TOOTHBRAKE FERN (*PTERIS DENTATA STRAMINEA*)** —This fern needs the same conditions as listed above.

BUTTERFLY PALM, ARECA PALM

BOTANICAL NAME: *Dypsis lutescens*

This palm is bright green with yellow stems. It's easy to grow, as long as it isn't overwatered, and is one of the top air-cleaning plants. Place it in a prominent spot because it is a beautiful focal plant for any room.

LIGHT PREFERENCE: A bright light is best, but without direct sun.

WATERING: Water thoroughly and allow the top of the potting medium to dry slightly before watering again. Use a well-drained potting medium, never allowing the palm to stand in water. Set the plant on a pebble tray to keep the humidity up. Dry air may not only turn the leaf tips brown, but also foster a spider mite infestation.

FLOWER: It has panicles of yellow flowers, but most likely not in the house.

SIZE: This palm may be up to 8 feet (2.4 m) tall.

PROPAGATION: Propagate by seed.

BUTTON FERN

BOTANICAL NAME: *Pellaea rotundifolia*

This is an endearing small fern with little leaflets that resemble small buttons. The leaflets grow from arching fronds with dark brown stems.

LIGHT PREFERENCE: Place this fern in a medium light. An east window is best, but a north window would also work.

WATERING: This fern does not want to be kept wet, but evenly moist. Water the fern, and let the medium dry down a bit before watering again.

FLOWER: Ferns do not flower.

SIZE: It grows 6 to 12 inches (15.2 to 30.5 cm) tall and wide.

PROPAGATION: The fern can be divided and potted up individually.

CAPE PRIMROSE

BOTANICAL NAME: *Streptocarpus*

Most often these cousins of the African violet are simply called *streps*. The clumps of long strappy leaves can be covered with flowers most of the year and are stunning. The flowers come in many colors and all are trumpet-shaped with a larger lip at the bottom. With the combination of colors on the flowers, they often resemble pansies.

LIGHT PREFERENCE: These grow well with African violets, as they need the same light conditions. Give them a medium light, such as in an east window or grow under electric lights for 10 to 12 hours per day.

WATERING: Keep the strep evenly moist. It would be better to err on the dry side than to allow them to stand in water.

FLOWER: The flowers rise above the foliage from 8 to 12 inches (20.3 to 30.5 cm). The trumpet-shaped flowers have three larger petals on the bottom fused to two smaller petals on the top. There are also some cultivars with double flowers.

SIZE: These plants take up a much larger area than the typical African violet. The leaves may spread 1 foot (0.3 m) or more.

PROPAGATION: The leaf of the strep can be used to propagate this plant in a couple of different ways. The leaf can be cut in wedges with V-shaped bottoms and placed V-shape down in a moist potting medium. The leaf can also be cut lengthwise, removing the midrib and taking each side of the leaf and laying it in the moist soil with the side that had been next to the midrib in the potting medium. Both of these procedures will result in new plants in a few weeks.

CULTIVARS: There are too many to list, but here are two easily obtained cultivars:

- **'YELLOW PINK CAP' AND 'YELLOW PURPLE CAP'**—Two newer cultivars in the gardening industry known for their two-tone flowers. Either pink or purple petals grace the top of the flower, while the lower petals are yellow.

CARRION FLOWER,
STARFISH FLOWER

BOTANICAL NAME: *Stapelia variegata* (syn. *Orbea variegata*)

The four-sided, leafless stems of this succulent are attractive and covered with prickly points on their edges. The "star" of the show, though, is the flower that appears, if grown in enough light. It's a star-shaped, taupe flower with splotches of burgundy all over the petals, with a middle shaped like a lifesaver and a smaller star shape in the center. This plant itself may not be exciting, but when it flowers, all that changes.

LIGHT PREFERENCE: Give this plant plenty of light if you would like to see these unique flowers. A south windowsill is perfect.

WATERING: Water thoroughly, and allow the potting medium to dry out a bit before watering again.

FLOWER: It produces a star-shaped yellowish flower with five petals covered in burgundy spots. The middle has a lighter-colored lifesaver shape with another star inside it.

SIZE: The plant will spread out as wide as the pot you put it in, but usually only reaches a few inches high.

PROPAGATION: Separate a piece of stem from the plant, allow it to callus over, and then pot in a moist medium.

CHINESE FAN PALM, FOUNTAIN PALM

BOTANICAL NAME: *Livistona chinensis*

The bright green leaves of this palm are almost completely round, unlike the more usual palm frond. These palms are a nice statement in a large room. In nature, they become quite large and form a single stem. In the home, that most likely will not occur and it will stay a many-stemmed small shrub.

LIGHT PREFERENCE: Give this palm plenty of light.

WATERING: Plant in a well-drained potting medium and keep evenly moist. Never leave it standing in water as it will rot the roots. As with most palms, dry air may encourage spider mites, so set them on pebble trays filled with water.

FLOWER: They can produce sprays of whitish-yellow flowers, but this most likely will not occur in the house.

SIZE: These palms can grow up to 50 feet (15.2 m) tall in nature, but will not exceed 10 feet (3 m) in the house.

PROPAGATION: The plant is propagated from seed.

CHINESE
MONEY PLANT

BOTANICAL NAME: *Pilea peperomioides*

This plant has taken the houseplant world by storm in the last few years. A petiole or stem that holds up the leaf is attached in the middle of the leathery leaf, adding to its unique character. These plants are usually passed from person to person rather than being bought. Even now, they may be hard to find to purchase, but are worth the search.

LIGHT PREFERENCE: Give it a medium light as an east or west window.

WATERING: Keep this plant evenly moist and increase the humidity by placing the plant on a pebble tray with water.

FLOWER: It grows small white flowers on pinkish stems.

SIZE: The plant can grow to 12 inches (30.5 cm) high by 12 inches (30.5 cm) wide.

PROPAGATION: Offshoots are sent up from the parent an inch or two from the stem. These can be separated and potted up individually.

When in dormancy, only water if the bulb is wrinkling and soft, in which case it could use a bit of water.

FLOWER: Small greenish-white flowers may appear in the spring.

CLIMBING ONION

SIZE: The bulb part of the plant can become large, up to 4 to 5 inches (10.2 to 12.7 cm) wide and may grow many offsets to become a cluster. The vine can grow many feet long, twining around whatever support it is given.

PROPAGATION: Remove the offsets, and pot up individually.

BOTANICAL NAME: *Bowiea volubilis*

This bulbous plant is easy to grow, if you are aware that the foliage will die down and the plant goes into dormancy in the fall. If not, you may think the plant has died and throw it away. In addition, the outer scales of the bulb turn brown like an onion, contributing to the idea that the plant is a goner. But it is only resting. Then, in late winter, a stem will appear from the bulb and begin to grow again. A trellis of some sort will be needed to support the large amount of greenery that appears. These bulbs can become quite large and remain solitary or can produce offsets.

LIGHT PREFERENCE: Give it a bright spot when the vines are growing.

WATERING: Water thoroughly and allow it to dry a bit before watering again. Do not let it completely dry out or it may drop the vines and go into premature dormancy.

CORSAGE ORCHID

BOTANICAL NAME: *Cattleya*

These beautiful flowers are the famous prom corsages of old. They aren't the orchid for beginners, but aren't too hard to grow and bloom as long as they have plenty of light. Keep them warm and give them a 10-degree drop in temperatures at night.

LIGHT PREFERENCE: These orchids need a lot of light to bloom. The leaf color is the indicator of whether the plant is receiving enough light. A light-green leaf means it has plenty of light; a dark-green leaf means it isn't receiving enough light to bloom. Place on a west or south windowsill, and if it still doesn't receive enough light, especially in the winter, it may need to be grown under electric lights.

WATERING: Plant the *cattleya* in a coarse orchid bark, letting it dry out a bit before watering again. Keep the humidity high by placing the orchid on a pebble tray.

FLOWER: The flowers are large and come in many beautiful colors. They are being hybridized for new colors all the time.

SIZE: They can range in size from mere inches to a few feet.

PROPAGATION: These can be divided, but only if they have more than seven stems.

CREEPING FIG

BOTANICAL NAME: *Ficus pumila*

These sprawling, small-leaved plants are perfect for covering a moss-stuffed topiary. The crinkled leaves come in dark green or white and green, and are often used as a groundcover in warm climates. Because of its thin leaves, it needs high humidity, so quite often you will find this creeper in a terrarium.

LIGHT PREFERENCE: Give it a low to medium light for the dark-green varieties. If the plant is variegated, it will need a brighter light to keep its variegation.

WATERING: Never let this plant dry out. It will drop leaves and may not recover. Do not let it stand in water, but keep it moist. Because it has thin leaves, it needs high humidity, so place it on a pebble tray.

FLOWER: This vine will rarely flower in the house.

SIZE: These vines grow almost flat to the surface of the medium but may spread many feet. Keep it pruned to control the size.

PROPAGATION: Take stem cuttings and insert in a moist potting medium.

CULTIVARS:

• **OAK LEAF CREEPING FIG (*FICUS PUMILA* 'QUERCIFOLIA')**—This small cultivar has leaves shaped like oak leaves, thus the Quercifolia name (Quercus is the genus name for oak trees). This tiny plant is quite often used as a fairy garden groundcover.

• **VARIEGATED CREEPING FIG (*FICUS PUMILA* 'SNOWFLAKE')**—This cultivar has a green leaf with white edges.

CROCODILE FERN

BOTANICAL NAME: *Microsorum musifolium*

The crocodile fern gets its name from the fact that the fronds resemble the skin of a crocodile. The long, wide fronds have a seer-suckered texture and are quite unique in the plant world. These are often found growing as epiphytes in their native habitat.

LIGHT PREFERENCE: A medium to bright light is best. This fern does well in an east window.

WATERING: Plant this fern in a well-drained, peat-based potting medium. Keep it evenly moist, but never standing in water. Place it on a pebble tray to keep the humidity high.

FLOWER: Ferns do not flower.

SIZE: Though this fern can get 4-foot-long (1.2 m) fronds in their native habitat, in the home they will rarely pass 2 feet (0.6 m).

PROPAGATION: These plants can be divided and planted up separately.

They come in shades of red, pink, white, and combinations of all three colors. They are constantly being hybridized to come up with more colors.

DESERT ROSE

SIZE: These plants can get large in their native habitat. They may be 2 to 3 feet (0.6 to 0.9 m) in the house but can be kept smaller by restricting the roots like a bonsai.

PROPAGATION: These can be grown from seed and from cuttings.

BOTANICAL NAME: *Adenium obesum*

The large swollen stem or caudex of this plant lends to its popularity. Leaves only grow at the tip of the stems, and bright, trumpet-shaped flowers appear there as well. The flowers range in color from red to pink and white, and the plant is being hybridized for more colors. These can be found as bonsai at many garden centers. Be careful when handling these plants, as the sap can irritate the skin.

LIGHT PREFERENCE: Give this plant as much light as you have available. A south window would be best.

WATERING: Plant this succulent in a fast-draining medium. Water abundantly during the growing season, as long as there is plenty of light and warmth. When the light levels are low and it is cold, do not water much, if at all. Never water them if it is cold where they are placed, as they will rot quickly. Never let them stand in water.

FLOWER: The flowers are the main attraction of this plant, along with the swollen stems.

EMERALD RIPPLE

BOTANICAL NAME: *Peperomia caperat* 'Eden Rosso'

The heavily corrugated leaves make this a unique plant. These leaves are held up on reddish-pink stems, adding to the charm. It may send up thin white flower stalks, which are interesting but not showy. Keep it in a warm area, and because it prefers high humidity, it is a good choice for a terrarium.

LIGHT PREFERENCE: A medium light is best, but this plant can handle low light as well. It also will grow well under electric lights.

WATERING: Plant in a well-drained potting medium, making sure the plant is never standing in water. Place on a pebble tray to raise the humidity.

FLOWER: The flowers are thin white spikes that resemble tiny rattails. The plant is mostly grown for its foliage.

SIZE: It can reach 8 to 10 inches (20.3 to 25.4 cm) tall.

PROPAGATION: Leaf cuttings can be taken and rooted in moist potting medium. Also, single leaves with a small amount of petiole left on can be potted in a moist medium with one-half of the leaf sticking out of the mix.

ENGLISH IVY

BOTANICAL NAME: *Hedera helix*

This is a popular vine, not only for its many sizes, shapes, and color combinations, but for its versatility. It can be used in a hanging basket, as a topiary, or framing a window.

LIGHT PREFERENCE: The plain-green varieties of ivy can tolerate low-light levels but prefer a medium to bright light if the plant is variegated.

WATERING: Plant your ivy in a well-drained potting medium. Water thoroughly and allow the mix to dry slightly before watering again. Never let it stand in water. An evenly moist medium is best for the ivy. If it is allowed to get too dry, the roots may die back and be unable to take up water when it is applied. This can lead to a complete collapse of the plant. Keep the humidity high around your ivy with a pebble tray, as dry air is like a neon sign advertising to spider mites to move in. When you do water the ivy, take it to the sink and use the sink sprayer as you water, which will clean the ivy leaves and deter spider mites.

FLOWER: This plant is grown for its foliage.

SIZE: Ivy can grow long stems but can be kept under control by trimming, or train it as a wreath or other topiary shape.

PROPAGATION: Take stem cuttings and pot in moist potting medium. The stems can also be pinned to another container of potting medium while still attached to the parent. Roots will form where the stem touches the moist medium. When the roots are established, it can be cut from the parent and grown on its own.

CULTIVARS: There are so many cultivars to choose from, with many leaf types, including tiny, large, green, yellow, green and yellow, green and white, and so many more. The variegated forms will need brighter light to keep the variegation. Find one, two, or three you like, make a topiary or frame a window.

- **'CURLY LOCKS'**—The solid-green leaves of this ivy are curled and twisted.

- **'GOLD BABY'**—The medium-green leaves have yellow edges.

- **'MY HEART'**—The leaves are heart shaped and dark green.

- **'SILVER DOLLAR'**—These green leaves are edged with white.

FALSE
ARALIA

BOTANICAL NAME: *Schefflera elegantissima* 'Bianco' (formerly *Dizygotheca elegantissima*)

This plant has an airy, fine texture as an immature plant. Each leaf has nine leaflets arranged palmately with ½-inch-wide (1.3 cm) leaflets when the plant is small, but as it matures the leaflets may be 3 inches (7.6 cm) wide. Each leaflet has a serrated edge, adding to the character of the plant; some say that it resembles cannabis. As it matures and the leaves become larger, it becomes a statuesque architectural plant.

LIGHT PREFERENCE: Place this plant in a medium to bright light.

WATERING: Plant in a well-drained potting medium. Water thoroughly and allow the medium to dry down a bit before watering again. Err on the side of dry rather than wet. Do not allow it to stand in water. Raise the humidity by placing the plant on a pebble tray.

FLOWER: The yellow-green flower umbels most likely will not appear in the house.

SIZE: This plant gets 25 to 50 feet (7.6 to 15.2 m) in its native habitat, but is a 3- to 10-foot (0.9 to 3 m) plant in the house.

PROPAGATION: These can be grown from seed, as well as from leaf and stem cuttings.

FIDDLE LEAF
FIG

BOTANICAL NAME: *Ficus lyrata*

There could not be a more popular houseplant right now. On every decorating show, every magazine spread, and countless Instagram accounts, you cannot miss this plant. Is it the plant for everyone, though? If you have soaring ceilings and the right conditions, yes. Its large, fiddle-shaped leaves and commanding presence make this a focal point in any room. This plant can be purchased in a shrub shape or tree shape, in many different sizes. The leaves are large and so collect a lot of dust. Keep them wiped clean so the plant can photosynthesize efficiently.

LIGHT PREFERENCE: Give this plant a bright light situation.

WATERING: Keep this fig evenly moist, not standing in water, but never dry either. Keep the humidity high by placing on a pebble tray.

FLOWER: Most likely it will not have flowers or fruit in the home.

SIZE: In it natural habitat, this plant can be a large tree. In the home, it can be 5 to 10 feet (1.5 to 3 m) tall and more, if you have room.

PROPAGATION: Use stem tip cuttings or air layering.

CULTIVARS:

- **'LITTLE FIDDLE'**—A much smaller version of the larger plant with leaves that may only reach 6 to 10 inches (15.2 to 25.4 cm) long.

FLAMING KATY

BOTANICAL NAME: *Kalanchoe blossfeldiana*

The flowers of this succulent are the main attraction. They come in red, orange, white, and pink, and are often sold as holiday plants, but can be found almost any time of the year. The succulent foliage is medium green with scalloped edges. Previously, these plants would be thrown away when they were done flowering, but after cutting back the spent flowers, they may send out sporadic blooms throughout the year.

LIGHT PREFERENCE: Give these succulents a bright light with some direct sun.

WATERING: Plant this succulent in a fast-draining potting medium. Water thoroughly, and let dry a bit before watering again. Do not let it stand in water.

FLOWER: The flowers come in many colors. Cut them back when spent. They may send out sporadic blooms throughout the year.

SIZE: These are smaller plants, ranging from 10 to 14 inches (25.4 to 35.6 cm).

PROPAGATION: Stem and leaf cuttings will root, but let them callus over first.

FRAGRANT
MINI ORCHID

BOTANICAL NAME: *Haraella odorata*

This miniature orchid is easy to grow and bloom. The tiny plant is only a few inches tall and wide, and it's often sold growing on cork or a small piece of wood.

LIGHT PREFERENCE: Give this tiny orchid good light to get it to bloom. A medium light in a west window is perfect.

WATERING: Soak your orchid once a week or more for approximately 30 minutes. Keep the humidity high, such as in a terrarium or hanging near a window in the kitchen or bathroom. If the humidity is low, it may need to be watered a few times a week.

FLOWER: The tiny flowers, approximately ½-inch (1.3 cm) high, resemble small, yellow-and-burgundy pansies. They are said to have a citrus fragrance, but are very small and hard to smell.

SIZE: This small plant is under 4 inches (10.2 cm) high and wide.

GREEN
WORM FERN,
E.T. FERN,
GRUB FERN

BOTANICAL NAME: *Polypodium formosanum*

The common names of this fern describe it perfectly. Its creeping rhizomes or modified stems resemble green worms or E.T.'s fingers. This plant is considered a "footed" fern: the airy, light green fronds arise from the green "feet."

LIGHT PREFERENCE: A medium light is best; an east window is preferable.

WATERING: Keep this fern evenly moist. If it is allowed to dry out, the fronds will begin to dry and fall off. Because of the succulent nature of the rhizomes, new fronds will grow if it is kept watered. Raise the humidity by setting the container on a pebble tray.

FLOWER: Ferns do not flower.

SIZE: The rhizomes will creep to the edges of the container, climb over the rim, and keep growing. A low, wide container is best for this creeping fern. The fronds will rise above the foliage approximately 12 to 18 inches (30.5 to 45.7 cm).

PROPAGATION: Take cuttings of the rhizome with a frond attached. Pin it to a container of moist potting medium with a florist pin or piece of bent wire.

HART'S TONGUE FERN

BOTANICAL NAME: *Asplenium scolopendrium*

This bright green fern has long, strappy fronds with wavy edges. Related to the bird's nest fern, it has a round grouping of fronds. The fronds are supposed to mimic the shape of a deer's tongue, thus the common name.

LIGHT PREFERENCE: Give this fern a medium light such as an east window.

WATERING: Keep this fern evenly moist. If it is allowed to dry out, it will lose leaves and the ends will dry out. Dry leaf tips may also occur from overly dry air. Place the fern container on a pebble tray.

FLOWER: Ferns do not flower.

SIZE: This fern will be approximately 1 foot (0.3 m) tall.

PROPAGATION: Propagate by spores or division.

HOLLY FERN

BOTANICAL NAME: *Cyrtomium falcatum*

The individual leaflets on the fronds of this shiny, bright green fern do resemble holly leaves. They have pointed notches along the edges, but are not related in any way to hollies. Because the fronds are a little bit leathery, this fern is more forgiving of dry air.

LIGHT PREFERENCE: Give this fern a medium light, such as an east window.

WATERING: Keep it evenly moist, not allowing it to dry out nor stand in water. Although it is forgiving of dry air, it would be better to set the fern on a pebble tray to raise the humidity.

FLOWER: Ferns do not flower.

SIZE: The fronds can be up to 2 feet (0.6 m) long, so the fern can be 4 feet (1.2 m) wide.

PROPAGATION: Divide by division.

IRON CROSS BEGONIA

BOTANICAL NAME: *Begonia masoniana*

The cross on the leaves of this begonia brings to mind the emblem seen on the shields of the Crusaders. It really adds interest to an already-unique, puckered leaf. This plant may start to lose leaves and seem to die right before your eyes. Fear not: it is most likely entering a time of dormancy, and leaves will reappear. Water just enough to keep the rhizomes plump during dormancy.

LIGHT PREFERENCE: A medium to bright light is preferred, but no direct sun. They also do well under electric lights. Too much light will bleach the leaves.

WATERING: Do not overwater this plant. It is a rhizomatous begonia, and the rhizomes hold water, so err on the dry side. Thoroughly water the plant, then allow it to dry out a bit before watering again. Keep the humidity high, and don't allow the plant to get cold.

FLOWER: They usually appear in the late winter, but are not showy, as the foliage is the star of this show.

SIZE: These plants may reach 10 to 12 inches (25.4 to 30.5 cm) high.

PROPAGATION: Remove a piece of rhizome and place in a moist potting medium.

JADE PLANT

BOTANICAL NAME: *Crassula ovata*

Also called a money plant or friendship plant, the jade plant is a popular houseplant and can become sizeable with bright light. It may be named "friendship plant" because of how often this plant is shared with friends. A single leaf can be the beginnings of a new plant and a friendship when you are gifted with one.

LIGHT PREFERENCE: Give the jade plant as much sun as you can. For best results, place it close to a south or west window. If it doesn't have enough light, it will have leggy, soft growth. In the winter, when the light levels are low, the times between watering will increase.

WATERING: Water thoroughly and let it dry a bit before watering again. Do not let it completely dry out as the leaves will pucker and drop off.

FLOWER: Star-shaped white flowers appear in clusters during the short days of winter if the plant receives enough light.

SIZE: If this plant has enough light and is well cared for, it can become a large specimen, up to 5 to 6 feet (1.5 to 1.8 m).

PROPAGATION: The jade plant can be propagated from a stem cutting or a single leaf. Allow both to callus over before planting in a moist potting medium.

CULTIVARS:

• **'GOLLUM'**—This is a popular cultivar, especially with kids, as its common name is "Shrek's Ears." The rolled ends do resemble his ears, or maybe the animator made his ears resemble the plant. Who knows?

• **'VARIEGATA'**—A cultivar that appears as if white has been melted into the green, leaving faded edges instead of crisp lines. The new growth may display some pink coloration as well.

JAPANESE FATSIA

BOTANICAL NAME: *Fatsia japonica* 'Spider's Web'

The large palmate leaves of this plant are striking. The fatsia can become a large plant and make a great focal point in a large area. If you have a cooler spot in the house, this plant prefers that, so it would be a perfect plant to greet your guests in a spacious foyer.

LIGHT PREFERENCE: Give it a medium to bright light to keep it more compact.

WATERING: Keep it evenly moist, reducing the amount of water in the low-light levels of winter.

FLOWER: White umbels of creamy flowers may appear, but they are unlikely in the home.

SIZE: This can become a large houseplant, 5 to 6 feet (1.5 to 1.8 m) tall.

PROPAGATION: Propagate from stem cuttings, but the large leaves may need to be cut in half to prevent the cutting from losing too much water as it roots. It may also be air layered.

KANGAROO FERN

BOTANICAL NAME: *Microsorum diversifolium*

This "footed" fern is different in that its rhizomes aren't overly fuzzy and are a dark chocolate color. The bright green fronds are deeply lobed. It's usually offered as a hanging basket; the rhizomes will keep growing until they spill over the rim and down the side of the container. They could completely cover the pot if allowed, or it can be moved into a wider pot. A low, wide pot is the best container for this fern.

LIGHT PREFERENCE: As with most ferns, it likes a medium light; an east window is perfect.

WATERING: Do not let this fern dry out, but keep it evenly moist and never wet. If allowed to dry out, the result will be yellow leaves that will fall off. It is a little forgiving because the rhizomes hold a bit of water. Keep the humidity up by placing the container on a pebble tray.

FLOWER: Ferns do not flower.

SIZE: The fronds rise above the rhizomes approximately 1 foot (0.3 m). The plant will spread as wide as the container it is in and beyond.

PROPAGATION: Remove a piece of the rhizome with a frond intact and pin it to a moist potting medium.

KENTIA PALM

BOTANICAL NAME: *Howea forsteriana*

A graceful palm native to Lord Howe Island near Australia, these slow-growing plants can be costly. But it is a beautiful palm to grow indoors as it has been since the 1800s. They grow naturally as a single-trunked plant but many believe that it suckers; when offered for sale, multiple plants have often been planted in one container. Place this palm in an east or west window and enjoy the exotic vibe it brings to your home.

LIGHT PREFERENCE: Give this palm a medium to bright light. It can tolerate a low light situation, but won't grow as full and nice.

WATERING: Use a well-drained potting medium and keep it evenly moist. Check the soil to see if it is dry. If it is, give it a thorough watering. In the winter, wait longer between waterings. Place it on a pebble tray to raise the humidity and prevent spider mite infestations. Take it to the shower many times throughout the year to give it a good rinsing off.

FLOWER: Creamy white flowers are produced, but not likely in the home.

SIZE: Although it may reach 40 feet (12.2 m) tall in its native habitat, in the home a size of 6 to 7 feet (1.8 to 2.1 m) is what can be expected.

PROPAGATION: It is propagated by seed, but this not a task the typical homeowner will have success with.

LADY PALM

BOTANICAL NAME: *Rhapis excelsa*

The lady palm has a completely different look than what one would picture when thinking of palms. The blunt-ended fronds are fan shaped with individual segments that naturally have uneven, ragged edges. The ends tend to brown: instead of cutting them with scissors, rip them to keep the uneven edge they naturally have. The stems have the added interest of a brown, mesh-like covering.

LIGHT PREFERENCE: The lady palm can tolerate low light, but prefers a medium light.

WATERING: Keep the medium evenly moist, never letting it completely dry out. If it is kept too wet, it may lead to root rot.

FLOWER: It mostly likely will not flower in the home.

SIZE: This palm can grow over 10 feet (3 m) tall if there is room.

PROPAGATION: The lady palm has offshoots that can be divided from the parent and potted up individually.

METALLIC PALM

BOTANICAL NAME: *Chamaedorea metallica*

This palm has unusual foliage: it has a blue-green sheen like a gunmetal finish. The individual leaves are split in the middle and fan out in a V-shape like a fish tail; it is sometimes called a mini fishtail palm.

LIGHT PREFERENCE: This palm naturally grows as an understory plant so can tolerate low-light conditions, but it prefers a medium light and is good for an office setting.

WATERING: This palm needs to be kept evenly moist.

FLOWER: It produces flowers and fruit, but may not in the house.

SIZE: This is a smaller palm at 5 feet (1.5 m) tall.

PROPAGATION: Propagate this plant by seed.

MOTHER FERN

BOTANICAL NAME: *Asplenium bulbiferum*

The mother fern is aptly named, as it produces small baby plants on its fronds. The fronds are lacy and the small plantlets make the plant a conversation piece. The babies are attached to small bulbils (small bulblike structures) that grow on the upper side of the parent frond. When they are large enough, they drop off, root, and grow on their own.

LIGHT PREFERENCE: Place this plant in a medium light, such as is afforded by an east window.

WATERING: Keep the potting medium evenly moist and the humidity high. A terrarium is perfect for this fern. Otherwise, place on a pebble tray.

FLOWER: Ferns do not produce flowers.

SIZE: The fronds can reach up to 2 feet (0.6 m) tall.

PROPAGATION: The small bulbils can be removed (or allowed to drop off on their own) and planted in a moist medium. Placing them in a glass container or covering with plastic works best when attempting to grow these small plantlets.

NARROW LEAF WAX VINE

BOTANICAL NAME: *Hoya kentiana*

The skinny leaves of this hoya cascade over the rim of the pot, making it a perfect small hanging-basket candidate. If it has enough light, it may produce clusters of dark pink flowers.

LIGHT PREFERENCE: A bright light is necessary for flowers to appear. A west or south window would be perfect.

WATERING: Hoyas can be kept on the drier side because of their thick, succulent leaves. Water thoroughly and allow the medium to dry a bit before watering again. It is better to err on the dry side than keep it too wet.

FLOWER: It can produce clusters of dark pink to burgundy flowers.

SIZE: This is a small hoya rising a few inches above the medium and cascading 10 to 12 inches (25.4 to 30.5 cm) down the side of the container.

PROPAGATION: Stem cuttings can be rooted in a moist potting medium.

CULTIVAR:

• **'VARIEGATA'**—The variegated form of this plant has touches of white and pink in the leaves, making it a handsome plant. Give it a good bright light to keep the variegation.

NERVE PLANT, MOSAIC PLANT, SILVER NET PLANT

BOTANICAL NAME: *Fittonia*

The nerve plant is grown because of its heavily veined leaves. Because they have thin leaves that prefer high humidity, a terrarium is a perfect environment. They come in pink, white, green, and red, and some even have piecrust edges. This endearing plant is also used often as a fairy garden plant.

LIGHT PREFERENCE: Medium light is best. High light will burn the leaves.

WATERING: This plant does not want to be too wet, as it will rot. On the other hand, do not allow it to dry out, as it will drop its leaves. Keep it evenly moist. This plant loves high humidity, so place on a pebble tray or in a terrarium.

FLOWER: It is grown for its beautiful foliage. If flower spikes appear, cut them off so all the energy can be used for the foliage.

SIZE: This is a low-growing groundcover up to 4 to 5 inches (10.2 to 12.7 cm) tall.

PROPAGATION: Tip cuttings root easily in a moist potting medium.

CULTIVARS:

- **'WHITE ANNE'**—This cultivar has green leaves with bright white veins.

- **'RED ANNE'**—It has green leaves with red veins.

- **'PINK STAR'**—It has green, ruffled leaves with pink veins.

NUN ORCHID

BOTANICAL NAME: *Phaius tankervilleae*

The nun orchid is often seen at garden centers these days and for good reason. It is a terrestrial orchid that is easy to grow in the house. It normally grows in the ground instead of epiphytically like most orchids. The flowers typically appear in January and February, and the hooded flowers resemble a nun's head covering. When the plant is done flowering, the foliage may look ragged or tired, and at that time may be cut completely down and new fresh foliage will appear. The blooms appear on new shoots the next year. The attractive dark-green leaves appear to have been pleated like a fan.

LIGHT PREFERENCE: Nun orchids need a bright light such as an east or west window.

WATERING: Keep well-watered but not standing in water. Use a coarse potting mix incorporating some orchid bark if possible.

FLOWER: The orchid is named for its flowers, which to some resemble nun's veils. They bloom on 3- to 4-foot (0.9 to 1.2 m) spikes in the winter months. The flowers are pinkish to peach to burgundy.

SIZE: The foliage is a couple of feet tall, but with the flower spikes, could be up to 4 feet (1.2 m) tall.

PROPAGATION: The clumps can be cut apart and each piece potted up individually.

PARLOR PALM

BOTANICAL NAME: *Chamaedorea elegans* (syn. *Neanthe bella*)

This palm has been used as a houseplant for generations. The tolerance to low light has been the main reason for its popularity. It grows slowly, and tiny versions of this plant are often used in dish and basket gardens.

LIGHT PREFERENCE: The parlor palm can tolerate low-light levels but prefers a medium light. If it receives too much light, it will turn a yellowish color. It normally is a bright green color.

WATERING: Keep the soil evenly moist but don't let the plant stand in water. Make sure to use a quality, well-drained potting medium. To lessen the chance of a spider mite infestation, keep the humidity high by placing the pot on a pebble tray and give a refreshing shower of water at least once a month.

FLOWER: If enough bright but not direct light is provided, the plant will produce tiny yellow sprays of flowers.

SIZE: This is a slow-growing plant, reaching 3 to 4 feet (0.9 to 1.2 m).

PROPAGATION: Propagate it from seed.

PIN STRIPE CALATHEA

BOTANICAL NAME: *Calathea ornata*

The beautiful foliage of this plant is its main attraction. It is often thought to be a prayer plant, and they are related. On the dark-green leaves, pink stripes feather out from the midrib to the edges on a slight curve. The undersides of the leaves are burgundy.

LIGHT PREFERENCE: Calatheas prefer a medium exposure to ensure the stripes stay a bright pink. Direct sun will fade the markings, yet too dark an exposure will not allow them to stay bright.

WATERING: Keep it evenly moist, not wet, but never dry. Place on a pebble tray to keep the humidity high. This is a must, as the leaf edges will turn brown if grown in dry air.

FLOWER: These plants are grown for their beautiful foliage and most likely won't flower in the house.

SIZE: It may grow to 2 feet (0.6 m) tall.

PROPAGATION: The calathea can be propagated by division.

STAGHORN
FERN

BOTANICAL NAME: *Platycerium bifurcatum*

This epiphytic fern has an imposing presence because of it large, antler-like fronds. These gray-green fronds rise out of non-fertile fronds and fork at the ends, giving them the appearance of antlers. The "antlers" are the fertile fronds, as they will produce the spores that can be used to propagate more ferns. The brown, papery, non-fertile fronds are the shield fronds that shield the roots that hold them tight to the trees they grow on. Staghorns are sold as small potted plants and often already mounted on a piece of wood, ready to hang on the wall like a mounted trophy. The brown fronds are often mistaken for dead parts of the plant, but they are not dead and should not be removed.

LIGHT PREFERENCE: As these naturally grow on trees, they are used to a dappled light, but not full sun. Give them a medium to bright light with no direct sun.

WATERING: Take your plant to the sink or shower and let the water flow on the rootball to ensure the potting medium or moss is completely soaked. Spray the green fronds as well. This may need to be done once a week or more if the fern is in a bright light. Do not allow them to dry out. If there is a place in the kitchen or bathroom for your fern with good light, they appreciate the added humidity.

FLOWER: Ferns do not produce flowers.

SIZE: These can become sizeable plants. If the shield fronds cover the piece of wood they are on, attach the wood they are growing on to a larger piece of wood.

PROPAGATION: They can be propagated by spores or by removing the smaller plants off the large parent plant.

STRAWBERRY BEGONIA

SIZE: The plant may be 6 to 10 inches (15.2 to 25.4 cm) high, but the plantlets can drape over the side of the pot one foot (0.3 m) or more.

PROPAGATION: The small plantlets can be detached from the runners and grown individually. They can also be pinned to a moist potting medium while still attached to the parent, ensuring they are getting water and nutrients while forming roots, allowing for a better chance to root and grow.

CULTIVAR:

• **'TRICOLOR'**—This cultivar has pink-and-white leaf edges.

BOTANICAL NAME: *Saxifraga stolonifera*

This plant spreads by growing baby plants at the end of long string-like stolons or runners. This growth habit gives it the common name strawberry begonia, though it is neither a strawberry nor a begonia. The leaves have silver veins on the dark-green, rounded, scalloped leaves; they have burgundy undersides. These small plants are perfect for mini gardens and also appreciate the high humidity of a terrarium.

LIGHT PREFERENCE: Give it a medium to bright light.

WATERING: Keep the potting medium evenly moist. Keep the humidity high by placing it on a pebble tray. If it is allowed to become dry or the humidity is low, the leaves will develop brown, dry edges.

FLOWER: Small flowers may appear above the foliage if in enough light.

WAFFLE PLANT

BOTANICAL NAME: *Hemigraphis alternata*

The leaves of this plant have the texture of seersucker material, all wrinkled and wavy. The color is a dark green with purple undersides. The whole plant is dark enough to make it seem burgundy. It's a welcome respite from an all-green palette in the houseplant grouping. In its natural habitat, it is used as a groundcover and spreads by stolons, which root along the way.

LIGHT PREFERENCE: Give the waffle plant a medium light such as an east window. Too much sun will bleach the leaves.

WATERING: Keep the soil evenly moist, but not wet or standing in water.

FLOWER: It has white flowers that are not conspicuous.

SIZE: This plant may reach 6 to 9 inches (15.2 to 22.9 cm).

PROPAGATION: Stem cuttings can be rooted in a moist potting medium or it can be divided into separate pieces and potted up.

CULTIVARS:

- **'SNOW WHITE'**—This cultivar has green foliage edged with pink and white.

- **'DRAGON'S TONGUE'**—The dark burgundy leaves of this cultivar are thin and strappy.

WHITE PEACOCK PLANT

BOTANICAL NAME: *Calathea* 'Fusion White'

This newer cultivar is grown for its brilliantly white variegation on dark-green leaves that have pink stems and light purple undersides.

LIGHT PREFERENCE: This variegated plant needs medium light to keep its variegation, but no direct sun, as the white part would burn.

WATERING: Keep the medium evenly moist and the humidity high by placing it on a pebble tray. Low humidity may make the edges and tips of the leaves turn brown.

FLOWER: This plant is grown for its amazing foliage.

SIZE: It will grow up to 24 inches (61 cm) tall.

PROPAGATION: Divide the plant into pieces and pot individually.

AFRICAN
MASK PLANT

BOTANICAL NAME: *Alocasia* 'Polly'

The oblong, triangular leaves of this plant do have an African mask vibe to them. Dark-green leaves with prominent white veins give them a distinct look. The key to keeping these plants happy is warmth, humidity, and never letting them dry out. If the temperatures are too low, the plant may go dormant until temperatures are at the level they need to grow again. If temperatures go too low, it may not come out of dormancy—ever.

LIGHT PREFERENCE: A medium light is best, as their natural habitat is the rainforest understory. They do not like direct sunlight.

WATERING: Keep the potting medium moist all the time during the growing season, but not standing in water. When the light levels are low in the winter, keep the medium a little drier. The humidity is the key, though. These plants will get a serious case of spider mites if the humidity isn't high. A pebble tray under this plant is a *must*.

FLOWER: If it were to flower in the house, it would display a green spathe with a white spadix.

SIZE: This plant is 1 to 2 feet (0.3 to 0.6 m) high.

PROPAGATION: These plants grow from rhizomes and produce offshoots. They can be separated and planted individually.

CROTON,
JOSEPH'S COAT

BOTANICAL NAME: *Codiaeum variegatum* 'Picasso's Paintbrush'

The colorful leaves of this plant are unbeatable. Hot, vibrant colors of red, orange, and yellow are the main colors on the dark-green leaves. The shapes of the leaves are also variable: thin and wispy to dangling and curling are just a couple of the unusual forms. These plants aren't terribly hard to grow, but it's tough to keep those vibrant colors bright in the house.

LIGHT PREFERENCE: Bright sun is needed for these plants to keep their color. A south or west window with some direct sun is recommended.

WATERING: Keep the potting medium evenly moist and the humidity high by placing the plant on a pebble tray. If the soil dries out, the bottom leaves will drop off. Low humidity will invite spider mites to take up residence.

FLOWER: Flowers can happen in the home with enough light, but they aren't very showy. This plant is grown for its fabulous foliage. The flowers are racemes of small, yellowish flowers.

SIZE: The croton can grow 3 to 6 feet (0.9 to 1.8 m) in the house.

PROPAGATION: Propagate it by stem cuttings.

CULTIVARS: There are so many cultivars, they all couldn't be listed here, but here are a few unusual ones.

• **'REVOLUTION'**—The leaves of this cultivar curl around on each other like corkscrews.

• **'DREADLOCKS'**—The long, strappy leaves are curly and droop down.

• **'HARVEST MOON'**—The dark-green leaves have yellow veins and midrib.

• **'PETRA'**—This cultivar is the most common variety sold. It has very colorful oval leaves that come to a point.

EYELASH FERN

BOTANICAL NAME: *Actiniopteris radiata*

This small, unusual fern is like no fern you've ever seen before. The fronds are fan-shaped and cut into thin sections. In nature, it grows in arid climates (compared to most ferns), so it needs to be kept drier than the typical fern, yet still never be allowed to dry out. It is an unusual fern and one that is worth trying.

LIGHT PREFERENCE: This fern, unlike others, grows in medium to bright light.

WATERING: Water well and allow it to dry out a bit before watering again.

FLOWER: Ferns do not produce flowers.

SIZE: This is a small fern, only 4 to 6 inches (10.2 to 15.2 cm) high.

PROPAGATION: Propagate by division or by spores.

FLAMINGO FLOWER, TAIL FLOWER

BOTANICAL NAME: *Anthurium andraeanum*

These plants grow as epiphytes, residing in trees, in tropical America. The spathes (modified leaves) are what most think are the flowers of the flamingo flower. They are heart-shaped and resemble patent leather or plastic. The flowers are actually called spadix and are the skinny, straw-shaped part protruding from the colorful spathe. The spathes come in many colors, from white to pink, purple, green, and orange and can last on the plant for months. They prefer warm, humid conditions to grow well, so never let the heat drop below 70°F (21°C) if you want this plant to be comfortable in your home.

LIGHT PREFERENCE: Give this plant a bright light, but not direct sunlight.

WATERING: Keeping it evenly moist is important, as is high humidity. They do not want to stand in water, though, so plant in a well-drained potting medium. It is best to use nontreated water; otherwise, the leaf tips will die back prematurely. It is imperative that they have high humidity, so keep the plant on a pebble tray. If there is enough light, keep it in the kitchen or bathroom where there is much more humidity than other rooms in the house.

FLOWER: The flowers consist of a spathe, the colored portion, and the spadix, which resembles a blunt-tipped rattail. The spadix may also be the color of the spathe or a cream color. The spathe is very thick and shiny, like patent leather and comes in many colors and color combinations.

SIZE: This is a medium-size houseplant ranging from 1 to 2 feet (0.3 to 0.6 m).

PROPAGATION: Divide the plant, and pot up the pieces individually.

FROSTY FERN

BOTANICAL NAME: *Selaginella kraussiana variegatus*

Not a fern at all, this plant is instead a club moss. The selaginellas are related to ferns, though, and like similar growing conditions. The white-tipped variety is often sold at holiday time and called the "frosty fern." These plants never want to completely dry out, so check them often. If the top of the potting medium feels dry, give it a drink of water. Because of its moisture and humidity preferences, the frosty fern makes a great terrarium plant.

LIGHT PREFERENCE: A medium light is best, as in an east window. These plants do not want to be in high light as it will bleach them out.

WATERING: Keep this plant evenly moist, never allowing it to dry out. If it is grown as a holiday plant, it may come in a decorative foil pot cover. Remove the cover when watering so that the plant is never standing in water. Raise the humidity by placing it on a pebble tray or grow in a terrarium.

FLOWER: It does not form flowers, but spores, like the fern family.

SIZE: This is a small plant only a few inches high, and it can spread quite far as it is a groundcover.

PROPAGATION: Propagate it by spores or division.

FURRY FEATHER, VELVET CALATHEA

BOTANICAL NAME: *Calathea rufibarba*

If you can't have pets in your home because of allergies, here is the plant for you. It is impossible to walk by this plant without running your hands up the back of the leaves. They are furry and soft, and it feels like you're petting a kitty. The topside of the plant is a bright green, but the soft, furry underside is burgundy, adding more interest to the plant.

LIGHT PREFERENCE: Give it a medium light, such as an east or west window.

WATERING: Plant in a well-drained potting medium, never allowing this plant to dry out completely nor stand in water. Keep the humidity high by placing it on a pebble tray, and, if possible, place it in a bathroom or kitchen where humidity is already a bit higher.

FLOWER: It most likely will not bloom in the home setting.

SIZE: It will grow approximately 1 to 2 feet (0.3 to 0.6 m) tall.

PROPAGATION: Propagate by division.

HEART FERN, TONGUE FERN

BOTANICAL NAME: *Hemionitis arifolia*

The endearing heart-shaped leaves of this fern rise up on wiry, dark brown stems. The fertile fronds grow on long stems, whereas the same-shaped, non-fertile fronds are closer to the potting medium on shorter stems. The look of this plant would lead one to believe it is not a fern or even remotely related to ferns. The leaves are stiff and leathery, without the small leaflets fern fronds usually have. This fern is often used for terrariums because of its need for constant moisture and humidity.

LIGHT PREFERENCE: A medium light, such as an east window, is best for this fern.

WATERING: Use a peat-based, well-drained potting medium, and keep it evenly moist but not standing in water. Place the container on a pebble tray or grow in a terrarium or under a cloche for best results.

FLOWER: Ferns do not produce flowers.

SIZE: This fern grows 6 to 8 inches (16.2 to 20.3 cm) tall and wide.

PROPAGATION: These can be propagated from the spores or by division.

WATERING: Plant in a fast-draining soil. Water during spring, but if you are questioning whether you should water, don't. The medium should never be completely dry, but never wet.

FLOWER: This plant flowers in the fall, but may not in the house.

SIZE: These plants rarely are more than 2 inches (5.1 cm) tall.

PROPAGATION: Propagate from seed.

LIVING STONES

BOTANICAL NAME: *Lithops*

If your watering regime errs on the side of not watering enough or consistently, these are the plants for you. Lithops will quickly die with too much water. These succulent, two-leaved plants naturally grow in the deserts of South Africa, and the resemblance to stones is their camouflage from grazing animals making a meal of them. The key to keeping them alive is not watering them, or watering extremely sparingly, from fall until spring. The new leaves begin to grow as the old leaves die, feeding off the old leaves as they shrivel up. They only ever have two leaves. The leaves vary in color and have interesting veins and blotches running through the leaf, often the same color but a darker shade than the base of the plant.

LIGHT PREFERENCE: Give this small plant as much light as you can, placing it on a west or south windowsill.

MAIDENHAIR FERN

BOTANICAL NAME: *Adiantum*

These delicate, airy ferns are one of the most beautiful of all ferns. The small leaflets on the fronds are fan-shaped with scalloped edges. The leaflets are thin and small, which is the reason they need such high humidity. If a window is available in your bathroom or kitchen, they love the elevated humidity. As long as you can provide this elegant plant with constant moisture and keep the humidity high, you can grow it.

LIGHT PREFERENCE: Place the maidenhair fern in a medium-light situation, such as an east window.

WATERING: The keys to growing this delicate fern is never to allow it to dry out and to raise the humidity. Place it on a pebble tray or grow in a terrarium for best results.

FLOWER: Ferns do not flower.

SIZE: These ferns can be 18 to 24 inches (45.7 to 61 cm) tall and easily as wide.

PROPAGATION: These ferns spread by rhizomes: a piece with a frond or two attached can be cut and potted separately.

NATAL LILY

BOTANICAL NAME: *Clivia miniata*

The long strappy leaves of the clivia are attractive, especially if they are the variegated variety, but when those large balls of bright orange or yellow emerge from the leaves, these plants are show-stopping. The key to getting them to bloom is the cold 40 to 50°F (4 to 10°C) treatment they need to be given for two months in winter, watering sparingly, if at all, during that time.

LIGHT PREFERENCE: Give the clivia a bright spot but not direct sunlight. Direct sun will burn the leaves.

WATERING: Use a fast-draining potting medium, never allowing the plant to stand in water. Err on the side of dry rather than wet.

FLOWER: Large umbels of orange or yellow flowers have been hybridized to include shades of orange, yellow, red, and light peach.

SIZE: These plants will reach 18 to 24 inches (45.7 to 61 cm) high.

PROPAGATION: These plants can be grown from seed, but it is much faster to divide the small plants from the parent and pot them up individually.

PEACOCK PLANT, ZEBRA PLANT, RATTLESNAKE PLANT

BOTANICAL NAME: *Calathea makoyana*

These plants are grown for their beautiful striped foliage; it brings to mind a zebra's stripes. The light green leaves have dark green stripes and spots on top and a burgundy color on the undersides. Use distilled or rain water for these plants, as the tips will brown from fluoride in treated water. Calatheas need even moisture and high humidity.

LIGHT PREFERENCE: Place in a medium to bright light such as an east or west window.

WATERING: Keep the humidity high by placing these plants on pebble trays and grow them in a bathroom or kitchen window where the humidity is a little higher already, if possible. Keep the well-drained potting medium moist, but not wet. Never let calatheas dry out completely. Dry plants and dry air, as well as fluoride in the water, can cause brown edges and tips on the leaves.

FLOWER: These plants are grown for their beautiful foliage.

SIZE: It will grow up to 2 feet (0.6 m) tall or more.

PROPAGATION: Propagate by division.

RATTLESNAKE PLANT

BOTANICAL NAME: *Calathea lancifolia*

The foliage of the calathea family cannot be beat. The tops of the leaves are speckled with dark-green spots and the undersides are purple. The humidity needs to be kept high for this plant to look its best.

LIGHT PREFERENCE: A medium light provided by an east or west window is best. Do not put it in too much sun or it may sunburn.

WATERING: Plant in a well-drained but peaty potting medium. It does not want to dry out and prefers a warm spot. Place on a pebble tray to raise the humidity.

SIZE: The leaves can grow up to 20 inches (50.8 cm) tall.

REX
BEGONIA VINE

BOTANICAL NAME: *Cissus discolor*

The beautiful leaves of this vine are dark green with a burgundy midrib and silver markings between the veins. The stems, petioles, and tendrils are burgundy as well. It really does appear that the leaves could belong to the rex begonia family, but the two plants are not related. Rex begonia vine needs moist, well-drained soil and elevated humidity to grow well. This vine is gaining in popularity owing to its use outside in shady combination containers. This makes it easier to purchase.

LIGHT PREFERENCE: Outside it needs a lot of shade, but as a houseplant it prefers a medium light to keep its beautiful colors bright.

WATERING: Keep it evenly moist in a well-drained soil.

FLOWER: This plant is grown for its foliage.

SIZE: The vine could grow up to 10 feet (3 m) long and require a trellis or hanging basket. It makes a beautiful wreath when trained on a vine or twig circle 12 to 18 inches (30.5 to 45.7 cm) in diameter.

PROPAGATION: Take stem tip cuttings and root in moist potting medium.

FLOWER: Small white flowers may appear if the plant receives enough light.

SIZE: These are usually sold in hanging baskets and may hang down many feet.

PROPAGATION: The vines can be propagated from stem cuttings potted in a moist potting medium, either with the ends stuck into the medium or the entire cutting can be coiled up and placed on top of the medium.

STRING OF PEARLS

BOTANICAL NAME: *Senecio rowleyanus*

This adorable vine should be called "string of peas" instead, but if you could picture the little succulent leaves being white, it would undoubtedly resemble a strand of pearls. The succulent, round beads are the modified leaves: these dangle over the edges of the pot and may send out small white flowers if enough light is provided. The easiest way to kill this plant is by overwatering. Err on the side of dry if questioning whether you should water or not.

LIGHT PREFERENCE: This succulent will need all the sun it can get in the home. Place in a west or south window so it receives some direct sunlight.

WATERING: The succulent little pearls store water, so plant in a fast-draining potting medium and water when the medium is quite dry. Do not overwater or allow this vine to stand in water. In the low-light levels of the winter, the time between watering will be much longer. Do not allow the medium to completely dry out or the pearls to shrivel.

37 Lifesaver Plant
(*Huernia zebrina*),
page 75

38 Lipstick Plant
(*Aeschynanthus radicans*), page 76

39 Lucky Bamboo
(*Dracaena sanderiana*),
page 77

40 Madagascar Palm
(*Pachypodium lamerei*),
page 78

41 Mini Monstera
Vine (*Rhaphidophora tetrasperma*), page 79

42 Mini Umbrella Tree
(*Schefflera arboricola*),
page 80

43 Mistletoe Cactus
(*Rhipsalis*), page 81

44 Money Tree, Guiana
Chestnut (*Pachira aquatica*), page 82

45 Moses in the
Cradle, Oyster Plant
(*Rhoeo spathacea*),
page 83

46 Moth Orchid
(*Phalaenopsis*),
page 84

47 *Neoporteria n idus*, page 85

48 *Neoregelia carolinae*, page 86

85 Sticks on Fire,
Pencil Cactus
(*Euphorbia tirucalli*),
page 123

86 Striped Inch Plant
(*Callisia elegans*),
page 124

87 Swiss Cheese Plant,
Fruit Salad Plant
(*Monstera deliciosa*),
page 125

88 Swiss Cheese Vine
(*Monstera friedrichsthalii*),
page 126

89 Teddy Bear Plant,
Panda Plant
(*Kalanchoe tomentosa*),
page 127

90 Trailing Watermelon
Begonia, Rainbow Vine
(*Pellionia repens*),
page 128

91 Tree Philodendron
(*Philodendron selloum*),
page 129

92 Umbrella Tree
(*Schefflera actinophylla*),
page 130

93 Variegated Saber Fig,
Banana Leaf Fig
(*Ficus maclellandii* 'Alii
Variegated'), page 131

94 Variegated Stromanthe
(*Stromanthe sanguinea*
'Triostar'), page 132

95 Variegated Wax Vine,
Wax Flower (*Hoya carnosa*
'Tricolor'), page 133

96 Veldt Grape
(*Cissus quadrangularis*),
page 134

145 Pin Stripe Calathea
(*Calathea ornata*), page 183

146 Staghorn Fern
(*Platycerium bifurcatum*),
page 184

147 Strawberry Begonia
(*Saxifraga stolonifera*),
page 185

148 Waffle Plant
(*Hemigraphis alternata*),
page 186

149 White Peacock Plant
(*Calathea* 'Fusion White'),
page 187

150 African Mask Plant
(*Alocasia* 'Polly'),
page 188

151 Croton, Joseph's Coat
(*Codiaeum variegatum*
'Picasso's Paintbrush'),
page 189

152 Eyelash Fern
(*Actiniopteris radiata*),
page 190

153 Flamingo Flower,
Tail Flower (*Anthurium
andraeanum*), page 191

154 Frosty Fern
(*Selaginella kraussiana
variegatus*), page 192

155 Furry Feather,
Velvet Calathea
(*Calathea rufibarba*),
page 193

156 Heart Fern,
Tongue Fern
(*Hemionitis arifolia*),
page 194

ACKNOWLEDGMENTS

Many people have been involved with the process of writing this book. I really don't know where to begin, except at the beginning. Thank you to my grandma, Elnore Eldred, who, though no longer with me, gave me the love for houseplants, especially African violets. To my parents, Keith and Christine Eldred, who raised us in the country and encouraged us to spend every minute we had outside, exploring the woods and meadows that surrounded our home. I can't say I loved working in the enormous vegetable garden that supported our family of six, but, looking back, I can certainly appreciate the time spent outside and nurturing plants. I watched my mom take care of her fern, given to her by my great-grandmother for her wedding shower in 1957, which she still has today. Many people have a piece of that fern, as my mom was always willing to share. I have had mine for thirty-two years. To my

brother, Keith, Jr., who spent the most time with me in the great outdoors and who also works with and loves plants. To my brothers, Brian and Kevin, who took such good care of Mom while I was unavailable and writing. Thank you.

To my best friend, Jeanine Merritt, who has been my biggest cheerleader through not only this book writing process, but through life. To Colleen Burton, Julie Smith, and Kathy Wilson, also wonderful friends and support systems. To my mutual houseplant friends, who are always up to houseplant shopping and have the same special skills of sneaking plants past husbands; Julia Hofley, Jean Mancos, and Sally Ouellette—you are the best. To my friend, Nancy Szerlag, who gave me the title of "Houseplant Guru" in the beginning, giving me the confidence I needed. To Bren Haas for all her support.

To all my friends in the Michigan Cactus and Succulent Society and the Town and Country African Violet club for not only their knowledge, but their friendships. To all the lovely women in the Hill and Dale Garden Club, who taught me much about gardening and became lifelong friends. To Penrith Goff from the Southeast Michigan Bromeliad Society for his conversations about bromeliads. To Jeremy Kemp from the Belle Isle Conservatory for his help and advice. Thank you to Shane Pliska and Lynn Allen for opening their homes for pictures. To Rob Halgren from Little Frog Farm for his lighting help. To George Papadelis at Telly's Garden Center, and Alyce and Richard Humphrey of Graye's Greenhouse, for allowing us to take photographs. To Dave Rocque for his help with palms.

A huge thank you to Elvin McDonald, who edited every word of this book and who has always been my houseplant inspiration. I was fortunate to meet him last year; it was an honor and I cannot thank you enough for all you have done.

To my heavenly Father for getting me through this project. I certainly could not have done it without much prayer and help from Him.

To my daughters: Chelsea, who collaborated with me on this project and added such beauty to the book, and to Hayley, who kept us both sane through this process. Thank you both for your support and love.

And last, but not least, to my husband, John; without his unfailing love and support in everything, I could not have accomplished this (and he only complains occasionally about the hundreds of plants that he shares his home with). I love you and thank you.

ABOUT THE AUTHOR

Lisa Eldred Steinkopf is the Houseplant
Guru, who features all things houseplants on her
blog, www.thehouseplantguru.com. She grew up
in rural mid-Michigan, where being immersed in
nature every day nurtured her love for the outdoors,
especially plants. Living down the road from her
grandma meant spending a lot of time watching her
grandma's lavish attention to her African violets and
other houseplants. This is where her love for them
began. Being an avid outdoor gardener as well has
led Lisa to write a monthly column and frequent
articles for *Michigan Gardening* and *Michigan
Gardener* magazines, respectively. In addition, she
has written for HGTVgardens.com, *Real Simple*
magazine, and the houseplant section of Allan
Armitage's Greatest Perennials and Annuals app.
Lisa has worked for over a decade as the annuals
and houseplants manager at Steinkopf Nursery, and
has been interviewed online, in print, and on TV
about houseplants. She is a member of numerous
plant groups, including the Michigan Cactus and
Succulent Society, the Town and Country African
Violet Society, and the Hardy Plant Society. She
cares for over 1,000 houseplants in her home in the
Detroit area, where she lives with her husband, John.
Lisa feels that every home, office, and apartment
should have a houseplant, and there is a houseplant
for every situation. A green thumb is something
anyone can have!

INDEX